Henry Coleridge Stuart

The Church of England in Canada, 1759-1793

From the Conquest to the Establishment of the See of Quebec

Henry Coleridge Stuart

The Church of England in Canada, 1759-1793
From the Conquest to the Establishment of the See of Quebec

ISBN/EAN: 9783337000721

Printed in Europe, USA, Canada, Australia, Japan

Cover: Foto ©ninafisch / pixelio.de

More available books at **www.hansebooks.com**

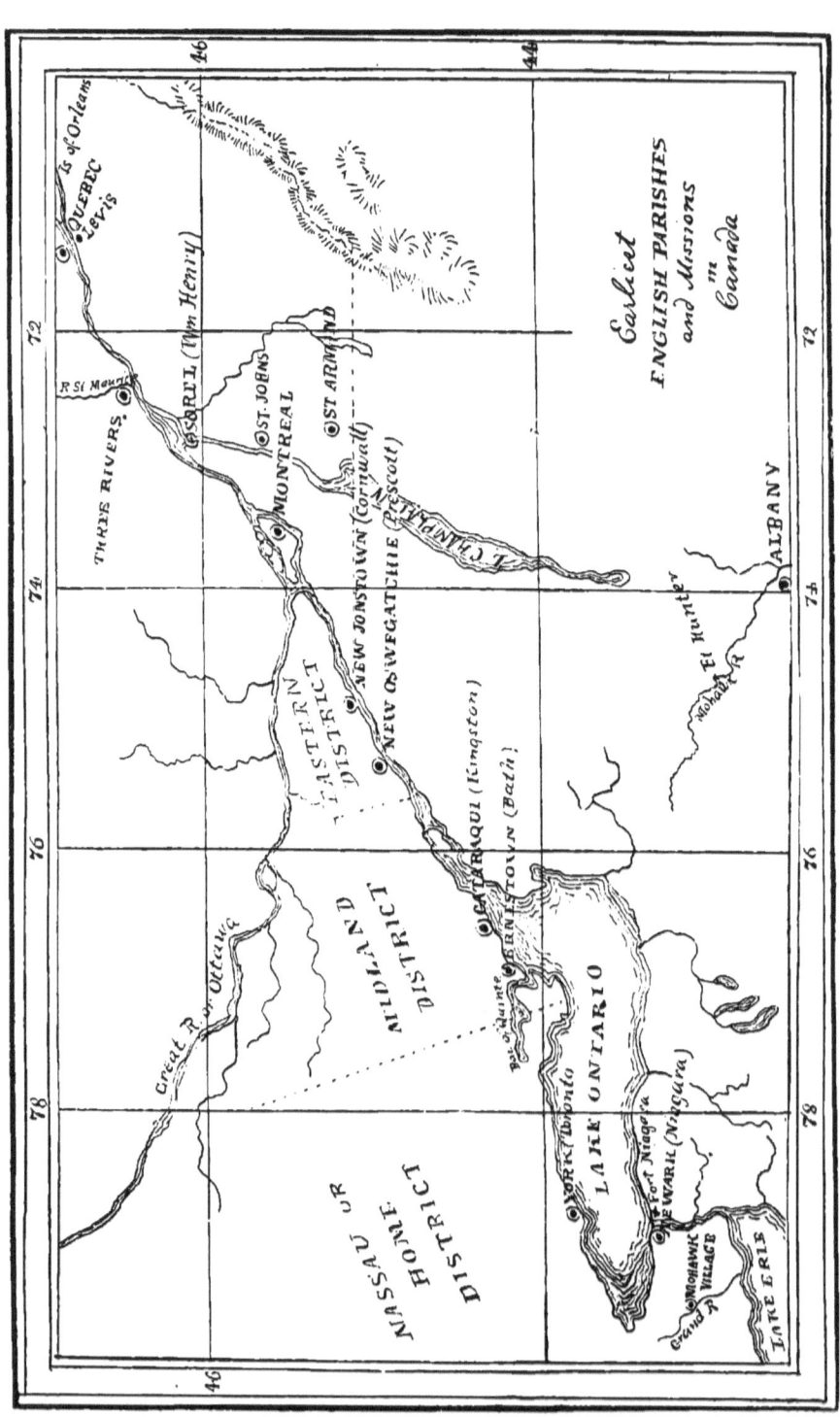

THE
CHURCH OF ENGLAND
IN CANADA,
1759-1793.

FROM THE CONQUEST
TO THE
ESTABLISHMENT OF THE SEE OF QUEBEC.

By H. C. STUART, M. A.,
RECTOR OF THREE RIVERS.

Montreal :
PUBLISHED FOR THE AUTHOR, BY JOHN LOVELL & SON.
1893.

Entered according to the Act of Parliament of Canada, in the year one thousand eight hundred and ninety-three, by H. C. STUART, M. A., at the office of the Minister of Agriculture at Ottawa.

CONTENTS.

	PAGES
MAP OF EARLIEST CANADIAN PARISHES....	
TABLE OF GOVERNORS, ETC....	4
INTRODUCTION....	5
CHAPTER I. UNDER THE MILITARY RULE....	7
" II. UNDER THE ROYAL PROCLAMATION	15
" III. THE THREE FRENCH CLERGYMEN	24
" IV. INFLUENCE OF THE AMERICAN WAR.	36
" V. THE THREE LOYALIST CLERGYMEN....	45
" VI. THE THREE ENGLISH CLERGYMEN....	57
" VII. THE BISHOP OF NOVA SCOTIA'S VISITATION....	61
" VIII. THE COMPLAINTS AGAINST THE FOREIGN DIVINES.....	78
" IX. THE CLERGY LIST OF 1790....	87
" X. THE CONSTITUTIONAL ACT OF 1791....	91
" XI. THE EPISCOPAL APPOINTMENT	101
" XII. CONCLUSION....	107

Governors of Canada.

AMHERST, GEN. JEFFREY.......
  Sept. 8, 1760, to ————
MURRAY, GEN. JAMES........
  Aug. 10, 1764, to June 28, 1766
IRVING, PAULUS ÆMILIUS.....
  June 30, 1766, to Sept. 23, 1766
CARLETON, LT.-GOV. GUY......
  Sept. 24, 1766, to Oct. 25, 1768
CARLETON, SIR GUY..........
  Oct. 26, 1768, to June 26, 1778

CRAMAHÉ, HECTOR THEOP.....
  Aug. 9, 1770, to Oct. 10, 1774
HALDIMAND, FREDERICK......
  June 27, 1778, to Nov. 15, 1784
HAMILTON, LT.-GOV. HENRY...
  Nov. 16, 1784, to Nov. 1, 1785
HOPE, LT.-GOV. HENRY.......
  Nov. 2, 1785, to Oct. 22, 1786
DORCHESTER BARON (Sir Guy Carleton), Oct. 23, 1786, to July 11, 1796

CLARKE, LIEUT.-GOV. ALURED......Oct. 11, 1791, to Sept. 24, 1793

Lieut.-Governors of Quebec.

CARLETON, GUY..............
  April 7, 1766, to Oct. 25, 1768
CRAMAHÉ, HECTOR THEOP...
  Aug. 24, 1775, to ————

HAMILTON, HENRY............
  ———— to Nov. 1, 1785
HOPE, HENRY................
  Nov. 2, 1785, to April 13, 1789

CLARKE, ALURED....................Oct. 8, 1790, to June 24, 1795

Lieut.-Governor of Upper Canada.

SIMCOE, COL. JOHN GRAVES................July 8, 1792, to July 20, 1796

Secretaries for the Colonies.

Appointed.
HILLSBOROUGH, WILLS, EARL OF.
  Jan. 20, 1768
DARTMOUTH, WILLIAM, EARL OF
  Aug. 14, 1772
GERMAINE, LORD GEORGE SACKVILLE..............Nov. 10, 1775
ELLIS, WELBORE......Feb. 24, 1782
SHELBURNE, WILLIAM, EARL OF..
  March 27, 1782
GRANTHAM, THOMAS, LORD......
  July 17, 1782

Appointed
NORTH, FREDERICK, LORD.......
  April 2, 1783
TEMPLE, GEORGE, EARL OF.......
  Dec. 19, 1783
SYDNEY, THOMAS, LORD.........
  Dec. 23, 1783
GRENVILLE, WM. WYNDHAM.....
  June 5, 1789
DUNDAS, HENRY.......June 8, 1791
HOBART, LORD...................
  March 17, 1801

Introduction.

THE story of the Church of England in Canada from the Conquest to the establishment of the See of Quebec has never been told. Possibly the reason for this is, that people thought there was nothing to be told, or, perhaps, nothing worth telling.

Almost nothing has been written on the subject, and that little has fostered this impression. The latest account professing to deal with the Church History of Canada thus settles this period in few words :—*

"The struggling settlers who gradually came in had to be content with such services as the garrison chaplains were able to give them.†"
"By 1781, the English-speaking population had increased to 6,000, and yet provision had not been made for even one clergyman of the Church of England ‡" "The American Declaration of Independence was made in 1776, and several years after this date there were only eight clergymen in Nova Scotia, and only one in New Brunswick; while in Canada there was not one.§" "There is no record of any visit ever having been paid by Bishop Inglis to Canada.||" "The unbroken forests everywhere covered the land, except along the shores of the sea, and the banks of the great rivers; so that it would have been exceedingly difficult and hazardous, if not impossible, to pass by land from the Nova Scotian to the Canadian part of his Diocese; while the journey by water would have involved a long sea and river voyage. The Bishop was, moreover, fully occcupied with the planting and supervision of the Church in Nova Scotia and New Brunswick; and for the present there seemed not much need for attempting to extend his ministrations to the regions beyond.**"

As a matter of fact, provision was made for several clergymen of the Church of England soon after the Conquest, Bishop Inglis did visit Canada, and the want of episcopal oversight was so apparent that the See of Quebec was established to meet that very want.

It appears to the writer that the story of the Church in Canada during those early years is worth telling. The need of episcopal

---
* Eastern Canada and Newfoundland. By Rev. J. Langtry, S.P.C.K., 1892.
† Page 40.   ‡ Page 41.   § Page 23 || Page 28.
** Do., page 39.

oversight, as shown in the abuses which hampered her progress, although it is painful reading, cannot safely be ignored. Then the particulars of the opening of the various Parishes possess an historical value, if none other. The visit of Bishop Inglis to Canada was a very important event. Its beginning and its ending were marked by an enthusiasm seldom witnessed in modern days. There were the acclamations of joy on the part of the populace, accompanied by the glitter of military ceremonial and the roar of artillery. And all along the line of his progress it was more like a march of triumph than an episcopal visitation. Equally interesting to churchmen should be the few particulars that survive of the lives of the early missionaries, the method of their appointment, and the sphere of their labours.

The sources of information for this sketch are the State Papers, Records of the War Office, Reports to the Society for the Propagation of the Gospel, Private Diaries, Parish Registers, Family Records, and especially the *Quebec Gazette*, the *Quebec Almanac*, etc.

The thanks of the compiler are gratefully tendered to the many who have assisted him in his work ; especially would he mention the name of Mrs. John Graham for kindly copying a number of papers now in the Canadian Archives at Ottawa.

ST. JAMES' RECTORY,
THREE RIVERS, August, 1893.

THE CHURCH OF ENGLAND IN CANADA.

1759-1793.

CHAPTER I.

UNDER THE MILITARY RULE.

1759-1764.

BEFORE the conquest of the country, the Church of England had been entirely unrepresented in Canada.

The first Anglican clergymen in Canada sailed up the St. Lawrence in June, 1759, or accompanied the land forces under General Amherst, as chaplains of the British forces. These were: John Lloyd, 15th Regiment; John Bourne, 43rd; Robert McPherson, 78th; Richard Kendall, 63rd; Michael Houdin, 48th; Ralph Walsh 28th; Lewis Bruce, 47th; Thomas Gawton, W. Nicholson, —— Jackson, John Ogilvie, Michael Schlaetler, 60th; Edward Whitty, 35th; and Henry Walker, 58th.*

Only two names in this list are brought into prominence in connection with their duties as chaplains. Michael Houdin, we learn from the S. P. G. Record, (pp. 55, 136, 854, 855, 869) was formerly a Roman Catholic Priest, ordained by the Archbishop of Treves on Easter Day, 1730. Subsequently we find him Superior of a Recollet Convent in Canada. Becoming a convert to the Church of England, he was duly received into the Church at New York on Easter Day, 1747. After some years of probation, he was appointed in 1753 to the Missions of Trenton and Amhill in New Jersey. The Record says that "he acquitted himself well" in this field. When the reduction of Canada was decided upon, Mr. Houdin attached himself to the British forces as chaplain to the 48th Regiment, and he was not only present at the capture of Quebec, but he materially assisted the besieging army, as General Murray specially mentions. On the 23d of October, 1759, he wrote from Quebec, intreating that his absence from his Mission might not bring him under the Society's displeasure, as what he had done had been in obedience to Lord

---

* This information was kindly furnished by the authorities of the War Office.

Loudon and other succeeding commanders, who depended much on his being well acquainted with the country. After the reduction of Quebec, he asked leave to return to his Mission, but the Governor, General Murray, ordered him to stay, telling him "there was no other person to be depended upon for intelligence of the French proceedings, and that he would acquaint the Society therewith." " He had," he said, " received a great loss by the death of the brave General Wolfe, who promised to remember his labour and services," and that he hoped to return to his Mission in the spring of 1760. He was detained, however, by General Amherst in Canada far into 1761, when he was transferred to the Mission of the French Refugees at New Rochelle, near New York. When writing about M. Montgolfier in 1763, General Murray stated that this priest had "had the assurance to write to a Monsieur Houdin, at that time chaplain to His Majesty's 48th Regiment, formerly a Recollet in this country."* As the letter referred to is lost, we have no means of ascertaining the nature of this communication which disgusted General Murray by its arrogance. As M. Montgolfier was at the time seeking the Quebec mitre, and seemingly satisfied with his prospects, we may suppose that his letter to the refractory Franciscan was altogether of an admonitory nature. Mr. Houdin retained the charge of New Rochelle until his death, which occurred in 1766.

The other name in this list to which special attention is given is that of the distinguished Dr. Ogilvie, the friend of Bishop Inglis. He remained in Canada until 1764, and his labours at Quebec and Montreal will presently be brought before us.

The British fleet sailed into the basin off Quebec on June 26, 1759. Whether we regard the English forces as mustering for prayers on the war-ships, or on the Island of Orleans, or near Point Levis, the first Anglican services in the country began in the vicinity of Quebec three months before the memorable battle of the Plains of Abraham, and the services thus begun have been continued without interruption to the present time.

Hawkins informs us that " The Rev. Mr. Brooke was the first clergyman who officiated in Quebec, although there is no record of his life or proceedings. He arrived, it is supposed, almost immediately after the Conquest. It was his wife who wrote the novel

---

* Kingsford's History of Canada, Vol. V., page 174.

ca'led 'Emily Montague,' the scene of which is laid in Canada."*

Dr. Brooke, however, informs us himself, in an early issue of the *Quebec Gazette*, that he had had regular services in the church during the summer of 1760, before the capitulation of Montreal.† When he wrote the letter referred to, he was greatly pained at the neglected state of the children of both soldiers and citizens, and he informs us that, in connection with General Murray, he memorialized the Society for the Propagation of the Gospel on their behalf, a movement which resulted in the establishment of a school. Dr. Brooke forwarded to the Society a list of names of children requiring assistance, and having authority to say that "the Governor would promote the endowment and good working of the school or schools by his personal contribution, and his constant countenance, and the weight of his authority."

A school was accordingly established. A sergeant ‡, willing and competent for the place, was induced to accept the post of teacher, and he continued to act in that capacity for one year at least, at the salary of £30 per annum, with a dwelling house provided for his own use.

We learn from the recently-published *Digest of S. P. G. Records*, that "the civil officers, merchants, and traders in Quebec," on behalf of all the "British Protestant inhabitants," appealed to the Society, in a letter dated August 29, 1761, in which the appointment of the Rev. John Brooke was solicited as missionary at Quebec. He had, the memorial states, "been personally known to many of them from the arrival of the Fleet and Army from Britain in 1757, and to all of them by their attendance on his ministry for more than a year past." And the petitioners promise to contribute to his support. General Murray thus refers to Dr. Brooke in his letter of Sep. 1st, 1761, in supporting the petition, which he did, he says, " in compliance with the unanimous request of the Protestants in his government," and " from a twenty years' knowledge of him and a particular attention to his conduct in the exercise of his functions for upwards of a year past." (S. P. G. Records, p. 137.)

In September, the British forces were increased by the arrival of the expedition despatched for the reduction of Canada. From the Province of New York, General Amherst, Commander-in-Chief,

---

* Annals of the Diocese of Quebec, by Ernest Hawkins, B.D., page 13. There is a copy of "Emily Montague" in the library of the Quebec Lit. and Hist. Society.

† *Quebec Gazette*, 13th Sept., 1764.

‡ Sergeant Watts, S. P. G. Records, p. 137.

was to conduct an army of 12,000 against the French positions on Lake Champlain, and thence to the valley of the St. Lawrence, whilst General Prideaux and Sir William Johnson were to lead their expeditions especially against Fort Niagara. These forces proceeded towards Montreal and Quebec, the former city capitulating on the 8th of September, 1760.

Amherst's colonial forces were soon afterwards sent back to New England and New York, but Dr. John Ogilvie, chaplain of the 60th Regiment, accompanied the commander to Quebec. This estimable clergyman was born in the city of New York. Having graduated at Yale College, and completed a course of training which fitted him for the sacred calling, he was duly ordained in England, and sent by the Society for the Propagation of the Gospel as a missionary to the Mohawk Indians at Fort Hunter in his native Province, in the year 1748. This mission had been opened by the S. P. G. as early as 1712, a church built, and the now historical communion plate, consisting of six pieces, all of massive silver, had been presented by Queen Anne for the sole use of "her Indian chapel of the Mohawks."* This plate and the fair linen which accompanied it were regarded by the Indians as the greatest of treasures. When Dr. Ogilvie arrived, he found that a Mohawk Sachem, known as "Good Old Abraham," had long acted as catechist to the tribe. During his ten years' sojourn at Fort Hunter, the Indians regularly attended the morning prayer which he read to them daily. In the year 1758, the Mohawks joined Amherst's expedition against Canada, and Dr. Ogilvie accompanied them as their chaplain. In this capacity he was present at the siege and capture of Fort Niagara in 1759. After the conquest of Canada, these Indians returned to the Mohawk Valley, where they remained until the close of the American war, when they finally emigrated to Canada, some to Lachine, others, in 1782, finding their way to the Bay of Quinté, and a favourable location a few miles from Newark, the present town of Niagara. Here they established themselves, built a village and a church. This structure Dr. John Stuart asserts was erected mostly at their own expense.

This event has not received the recognition it deserves, but there appears to be abundant evidence that whilst the English residents of Eastern Canada were complaining of the Government's remiss-

---

* Pascoe's Digest of S. P. G. Records, page 165.

ness in providing them with places for public worship, to the Mohawk warriors belongs the honor of erecting, mostly at their own expense, THE FIRST PROTESTANT CHURCH ERECTED IN CANADA AFTER THE CONQUEST.

Subsequently the Government purchased a tract of land on the Grand River, about ninety miles west of Niagara, to which the greater number of the Six Nations then in Canada repaired. The Mohawk church, which still stands near Brantford, was built by the Government in the year 1785. This structure, although contemporary with the church at Sorel, was the second Indian church erected in this country.*

Dr. Ogilvie says that during the campaign of 1759, the Mohawks attended the church services regularly. He was, he says, an eye-witness of many evidences of the humanizing and spiritualizing power of Christianity among the Mohawk warriors, such as "would have been a noble subject for the pen of one of the Jesuits of Canada," and which he describes with great simplicity. It was indeed to the principles of truth thus faithfully given and received, that we must attribute the undeviating loyalty of the Mohawks to the British Crown—they alone, of all the Indian tribes, continuing steadfast.† Dr. Ogilvie reminds us that Indians are shrewd observers, and that it did not escape their notice at Fort Niagara, that whilst the French had provided all the Indian nations from Canada to the Mississippi with priests and decent places of worship, the British Protestants presented a striking and shameful contrast. "The Indians themselves," he says, "were not wanting in making pertinent reflections] on the inattention of Protestants on these points."‡ Writing of the prospect of tranquillity after the capture of Quebec, he expressed his "deep thankfulness that there was no more leading into captivity, no more complaining in their streets, and his earnest desire was that " the Conquest might lead to the wider and more rapid spread of the knowledge of the only true God, and Jesus Christ whom He hath sent."§

At general Amherst's express command, Dr. Ogilvie assumed the charge of the congregation at Montreal during the winter of 1760.‖ Subsequently he returned to Quebec where he remained

---

*A picture of this church is contained in the Canadian Church Magazine for January, 1892.
† Anderson's History of the Colonial Church, Vol. III., pp. 431-2.
‡ S. P. G. Annual Report for 1761.
§ Hawkins' Annals of the Diocese of Quebec, p 283.
‖ S. P. G. Record, p. 136.

until 1763, labouring in conjunction with Dr. Brooke. Not only did he faithfully attend to the duties devolving upon him as chaplain of his regiment, like reading publicly the daily offices of morning and evening prayer, but he also undertook some special French work in the neighbourhood of Quebec. He went among the French Canadians, mixing freely with them, and, we are expressly told, met with surprising success in this work, even establishing " numerous congregations " among them and making many converts from the Church of Rome.*

Having laboured in this field for four years, Dr. Ogilvie, with his regiment, was transferred to Montreal. Here he was commissioned to officiate in the double capacity of chaplain of the forces, and first incumbent of the "Parish of Montreal." He says that " The British merchants with the garrison in Montreal made a considerable congregation, who assembled regularly for Divine Worship on Sundays and other Festivals ;" that from Nov. 1760 to July 1763 he baptized 100 children, and administered the Holy Communion to 30 or 40 persons at a time; and that they were obliged to use a Roman Catholic chapel for their services.‡ The duties of his new post requiring all his attention, he was unable to prosecute the French work, so successfully carried on at Quebec. Being painfully impressed by the deplorable state of the people, he wrote to the Society on the subject, but owing probably to the low state of funds, the subject of French evangelization was deferred Having laboured at Montreal for one year, in 1764 he returned to New York city, where he became one of the assistant ministers of Trinity Church. Here, as hitherto, success followed his ministrations. We are told that he was especially celebrated " for the power with which he secured the love and confidence of those who sought his counsel in private conference, and for the lucid and impressive manner in which he expounded the Scriptures in his public lectures."† " He was still exercising, in the strength of matured manhood, the best energies of his mind, and might have thought that length of days was before him, when death arrested his career. A stroke of apoplexy fell upon him in the pulpit, just after he had recited the text of a sermon which he was about to preach ; and the

* S. P. G. Annual Report for 1783.
† Berrian's History of Trinity Church, pp. 132-4.
‡ S. P. G. Records, p. 136.

few brief days in which his spirit yet lingered within its shattered tabernacle were enough to prove his cheerful submission to the will of God.*"

He had been assistant-minister at Trinity Church for nine years, dying in 1774. It is of no little interest to Canadian churchmen that his fellow-labourer during those last blessed years of his life was none other than his dear friend, Charles Inglis, who was consecrated, a few years later, to the See of Nova Scotia, and became the first Colonial Bishop of the Church of England. Indeed it is to Dr. Inglis's address at the funeral of his friend that we are indebted for the closing particulars of Dr. Ogilvie's life.†

The Articles of Capitulation specify that, "The free exercise of the Catholic, Apostolic and Roman religion shall subsist entire, in such manner that all states and people of the towns and country-places, and distant posts, shall continue to assemble in the churches, and to frequent the Sacraments as heretofore, without being molested in any manner, directly or indirectly. These people shall be obliged, by the English Government, to pay to the priests the tithes and all the taxes they were used to pay under the Government of his most Christian Majesty."

The answer was, "Granted, as to the free exercise of their religion. The obligation of paying the tithes to the priests will depend on the King's pleasure." The words at Montreal were [Article 27], "Accordé pour le Libre Exercice de leur Religion," and at Quebec [Article 6], "Libre exercise de la Religion Romaine Sauvegardes accordes." The Articles of Capitulation were drawn up in French only.

The various Roman Catholic churches in the towns of Quebec and Montreal appear to have been seized and at first utilized as receptacles for government stores. The Canadians, however, in accordance with the Articles of Capitulation, were permitted to hold their religious services in them, with this difference, that instead of worshipping in them as virtual owners, they were now permitted to enter them and make use of them on sufferance only.

Not long after the Conquest, there were a sufficient number of British residents at both Quebec and Montreal to constitute a *Parish*. Numbers of people are always found ready to follow in

---

* Anderson's History of the Colonial Church, Vol. III. page 600.
† Anderson's History of the Colonial Church, Vol. III., page 600.

the wake of an army, and there was no exception to the rule in the case of the British invasion of Canada. At first, the number was small. Traders and adventurers were the first to come, and so rapidly did they increase that, in 1764, General Murray estimated their numbers as more than 1,400 " strangers" in Quebec alone.*

At the close of the Military Rule, in the year 1764, we find two Parishes virtually established. That of Quebec dating from 1760, and under the pastorate of Dr. Brooke, and that of Montreal dating from 1763, and under the incumbency of Dr. Ogilvie. The services at Quebec were held at the Recollet Church, and at Montreal at the Chapel of the Ursulines—limited, however, to one hour's duration every Sunday morning.†

---

* Kingsford's History of Canada, Vol. IV., page 413, note.
† Additional Papers concerning Quebec, Dec., 9, 1775, p. 149.

CHAPTER II.

UNDER THE ROYAL PROCLAMATION.

1764-1774.

THE Treaty of Paris was signed on the 10th of February, 1763. By this instrument, "His most Christian Majesty and the Crown of France" renounced all pretentions to Canada, guaranteeing all rights to the same to the King and Crown of Great Britain. On the 7th of October, in the same year, a Royal Proclamation was issued, establishing Quebec as a British Province. The Proclamation, however, did not reach Quebec until the 10th of August, 1764. When it arrived, General Murray assumed the government, and the military rule, which had been followed since the Conquest, came to an end.

The clause referring to the Roman Catholic Church in Canada is contained in the 4th Article, and is as follows :—

"His Britannic Majesty, on his side, agrees to grant the liberty cf the Catholic religion to the inhabitants of Canada: he will consequently give the most effectual orders that his new Roman Catholic subjects may profess their religion according to the rites of the Roman Church, as far as the laws of Great Britain permit." The last clause of this Article was afterwards interpreted with respect to the religious orders of men, namely, the Jesuits and Recollets, that no novices should be received by them. They should continue to enjoy all the benefits of their property during the period of their lives; but, when the last survivor of each order died, the estates of these religious orders should pass to the Crown.

With regard to the privileges accorded to the British settlers, the Proclamation expressly declared, "That as soon as the state and circumstances of the said Colonies will admit thereof, they shall, with the advice and consent of the Members of our Council, summon and call General Assemblies within the said Governments respectively in such manner and form as is used and directed in those Colonies and Provinces in America which are under our immediate government; and we have also given power to the said governors, with the consent of our said Councils and Representatives of the people, so to be summoned as aforesaid, to make, constitute and ordain Laws, Statutes, and Ordinances for the public peace, welfare and good government of our said Colonies, and of the people and inhabitants thereof, as near as may be agreeable to the Laws of *England*, and under such regulations and restrictions as are used in other Colonies ; and in the meantime, and until such assemblies can be called as aforesaid, all persons inhabiting in or resorting to our said Colonies, may confide in our royal protection for the enjoyment of the benefit of the Laws of 'our Realm of England ; for which purpose, we have given power under Our Great Seal to the Governors of Our said Colonies, respectively, to erect and constitute, with the advice of our said Councils, respectively, courts of Judicature and public justice within our said Colonies, for the hearing and determining all causes, as well criminal as civil, according to Law and Equity, and as near as may be, agreeable to the Laws of England, with liberty to all persons, who may think themselves aggrieved by the sentence of such courts, in all civil cases to appeal, under the usual limitations and restrictions, to us in our Privy Council."

This part of the Proclamation became speedily the cause of much trouble in the new colony, and led eventually to the recalling of General Murray. Having resided for five years among the French Canadians, Murray had learned to value them, and with all his soul to detest the narrow view held by so many of the British settlers, that the new subjects had no rights they were bound to respect. The question concerning the civil rights of the new subjects became at once the burning question of the day. Murray, and after him Carleton, openly espoused the side of the French, whilst the British residents of the country, a powerful society of London merchants, and the whole nation generally, were ranged on the other side.

Dr. Brooke was looked upon by many of the dissatisfied British residents as deep in the counsels of the governor, and he was distrusted accordingly. The following letter, published in the *Quebec Gazette* of the issue of the 16th August, 1764, probably owes its existence to this state of public feeling :—

" The most unhappy condition of the poor children of this Garrison, especially those of the Army, for Want of Learning, calls for the Consideration and Assistance of Government, and of every opulent British Subject, to point out the Means by which they may obtain necessary Education. To see them strolling in the streets like abandoned Miscreants, blaspheming the most sacred Name of their Maker, and lisping Curses and Imprecations ere their Legs can scarce support their tender Frames, is shocking to human Nature, and a Reproach to the Country they live in. The exorbitant Price demanded by those who keep Schools, renders it impossible for the unhappy Parent to procure them the most necessary and inestimable Qualification of Reading; which consequently must cause Self-Accusation, as Zeal for the Country, in entering the Service, has lost their Share of the charitable Donations so liberally distributed at Home for the Education of Children. I remember a Contribution was made in the Church last Summer, said to be for that charitable Use, but never could learn of any who benefitted thereby. I humbly presume if a Proposal of that kind was made by some Person of Rank, and spirited by every good Person, a Provision might be made for the Education of such miserable Objects.

"Every Person must be sensible, in some Degree, of the Permanency and universal Utility of Learning; how necessary to instruct and inculcate in the Mind the true Notions of Religion, and by the Frequency of its Applications to renew the same; how entertaining in Solitude, consolatory in Adversity, and how absolutely necessary in Business of all kinds. To point its intrinsic Value, and the most unhappy Condition of those who, from its Want, have little to humanize their minds, and nothing but external Objects, and the too frequent Examples of Vice to spur the noble Faculty of Thought, requires a more able Head than mine, therefore humbly recommend it to the wise Consideration of Government, and the British in General."

To this letter, Dr. Brooke rejoined in the issue of the 18th of October. We can forgive the half-veiled insinuations of the foregoing epistle, on account of the gentlemanly letter it called forth from the chaplain of the garrison, and first Incumbent of Quebec, every word being very precious in the picture it gives us of the period in question.

"There appeared in your Paper of the 16th, past, a Complaint with Respect to the Children of the Soldiery and other Poor, with an Admonition to take Measures for the Redress of it, in which I believe every good Man will readily agree with the Author. But by his Manner of writing, he seems to have been unacquainted, that, as far as the state of things admitted, all proper Steps to the Purpose, had been taken from our first being in peaceable Possession of this Capital. In the year 1760, the Society at Home was wrote to for Assistance by the Governor himself, and the case of the children of the Poor represented at large, with an Estimate of their Number, in a Letter from me, writing under his Authority, and assuring that venerable Body that he would promote the Settling and Endowment of a School, or Schools, as should be found needful, by his personal Contribution, as well as the Countenance of his Authority. In the Interim, till the Society's Determination should be known, a Sergeant, one who was thought best qualified for the Employment of any Person that could be found willing to undertake it, was excused Duty, appointed School-Master, had a Place allowed him for Dwelling and School, and was to have 30*l.* per Annum, Salary, one year of which I am authorized to say he received: And more he might have received, but for his growing remiss in his Attention: and the Soldiers and others in sending their Children: the Consideration for this Appointment therefore ceasing, it consequently was discontinued. I cannot agree with the Author, in allowing the Price demanded by the English who kept School here, to be exorbitant: It is indeed too heavy for the poorer kind of People to pay; but yet far from keeping Pace with the superior Rates at which all things stand here to what they do in England or the other Colonies.

" The few we have in this Employment scarcely make out a Support; and, as I am informed, they would have little prospect, if they abated of their Price, of making it up by Numbers, those who are capable of paying anything for their Children being so [doing so?] at the present Rate. But however this may be, in Consequence of the Steps already taken, the Society is disposed to give its Assistance, and a Provision for the Education of the Children of the Poor will undoubtedly be settled, as soon as the Nature of our Situation with respect to the Mother-Country, and other Circumstances will admit. As to the Collection made for a few Sundays at Church last year, it amounted to but an inconsiderable Sum, and though the gentleman never heard that any of it was applied to the Schooling of Children, he might have heard it, would he have enquired where Information was to be had; had he taken this Method, he would have saved himself the Trouble, by his Publication in your Paper, of giving People that are Strangers to us but very indifferent Impressions concerning us, and me that of setting them right. It is now seen that there has been no Neglect of so truly important a Concern: And if the Gentleman, or any other Person, will cal upon me, I am ready at any Time to satisfy them that I have expended much more than ever was collected for the Uses the Collection was made, which was for such charges as necessarily attended the keeping up of public Worship, for Relief of very needy Objects and the like, and never was declared to be for the Schooling of Children only; besides which my Note of Hand is now standing against me, to *Mr. Samuel Gridley*, Merchant, for Thirty-two Pounds, Currency, and upwards, advanced by him for benching the Church, and for a Funeral Pall, which I was directed by several Gentlemen of the Place to have done on the Assurance they would readily be paid for by Subscription, but as yet seem to rest on me. When the public-spirited Author of the Letter comes to know this, I hope he will subscribe very handsomely towards easing me of this Burden, and I assure him that neither my Subscription, nor any other Aid I can give, shall be wanting to establish a School for the Poor, to the Care of it when established, or any other scheme of public utility. At the same Time, the Letter-Writer must excuse me for observing, that every Person who could be concerned in any Thing his letter relates to, must have been perpetually accessible to him, for whatever Time he has been an Inhabitant of the Place. The Candid and becoming Part, therefore, would have been, his applying to all such personally: Nor could it have been less effectual towards promoting the good work which he appears so zealous for. The Part he has chosen, has been that of addressing himself to the Public, in a Paper that may circulate through all His Majesty's Dominions, upon Presumption instead of Information ; and by this to create unfavorable Surmises as to Persons and Measures, with Respect to both which, I hope it now appears, there hath been no culpability, either by Neglect or otherwise. However, as I have received no information concerning the Letter-writer, so I have not taken the Liberty so much as to conjecture who he is. Notwithstanding Appearances, he may have no malignant Intention, and on the Supposition he has not, I am his

Very humble Servant,
J. BROOKE."

In October, 1764, the first Quarter Sessions Grand Jury which assembled in Canada met at Quebec. It is asserted that the duties of this body appear never to have been more misunderstood than on this occasion.* This Grand Jury at once proceeded to draw up *Articles of Presentment*, arranged under fifteen heads. The Seventh

---

* Kingsford's History of Canada, Vol. V , page 153.

Article drew attention to the fact that "The better observance of the Sabbath was called for: so that it should not be profaned by selling, buying, keeping open shop, balls, routs, gaming, or other idle diversions, and that a learned clergy was required to preach the Gospel in both languages." The last clause of this Article was doubtless aimed at Dr. Brooke's inability to continue the French work so ably carried on by Dr. Ogilvie.

This body then proceeds to more extravagant demands, as that the Grand Jury should be consulted before any ordinance of the Government should become law, and that the public accounts should be laid before it at least twice a year. Their chief grievance, however, was set forth in a special supplemental clause. This was that persons professing the Religion of Rome, and recognizing the Supremacy of the Pope, were sworn and allowed to act as jurors, when they were disabled from holding any office of trust or power by Act 3, James I., Cap. 5; and that such men, therefore, being named jurors, acted in open violation of "our most sacred laws and liberty, tending to the entire subversion of the Protestant religion and his Majesty's authority."

This was a very serious accusation. But the Governor was not a man to be caught napping. Certain men, whose names were attached to the presentment, claimed that when signing the document, they were unaware of the nature of the Articles in question. A counter petition was accordingly drawn up containing the signatures of these men.

In answer to this serious charge, Murray pleaded the fact that the laws of England did not permit him to act otherwise than he had done, as there were not in the whole Province ten Protestants who were qualified by the laws of England to act as jurors. To counteract the assertion that there were thousands of Protestants in Canada, Murray caused to be prepared and forwarded to England, lists of the Protestant house-holders of the towns of Quebec and Montreal, few of whom, however, were free-holders.

These lists are of great consequence as marking the great need for the early establishment of the first two English Parishes in Canada, and I must beg the reader's indulgence for giving them in full.

A List of Protestant House-Keepers in Quebec, Oct. 26, 1764.

Councillors :—([1]) Thomas Dunn, Francis Mounier, Benjamin Price.

Justices of the Peace.—Thomas Ainslie, (⁵) John Grant, Samuel Gridley, Joseph Walker, Hugh Finlay, Peter Traverse, (¹⁰) Richard Murray, John Martell, Frans. Jeveck, John Collins, John Row, (¹⁵) Thomas Story, John Gray.

Housekeepers.—James Potts, John Elliott, Peter Fennil, (²⁰) James Jeffreys, John McCord, Will Govett, Gustian Franks Joseph Mattier, (²⁵) John Gustineau, Jno. Lymburner, John Lee, Alexr. Simpson, George Fulton, (³⁰) Simon Fraser, John Barnard, Alex. Dumas, William Mackenzie, Robert McPhee, (³⁵) Robert Hunter, Isaac Warden, Henry Mounier, David Algie, Edward Watts, (⁴¹) John Beack, Charles Grant, John Patterson, Thomas Winter, Samuel March, (⁴⁵) Alexr. McKenzie, John Bondfield, John Wasmoor, John Phillips, Acklon Bondfield, Jeremiah Condy Russel, Benj. Jacount, Stephen Moor, John Danver, James Brookes, (⁵⁵) James Aitkins, Thomas Seaney, Samuel Sills, Will. Grant, Calvin Gage, (⁶⁰) George Alsop, James Shepherd, James Johnston, John Purse, Stephen Badsley, (⁶⁵) Peter Napier, John Malcolm, George Jenkins, Christopher Spring, George Milner, (⁷⁰) Jacob Dessan George McAdam, James St. Clair, John Taylor, Will Abbott, (⁷⁵) Samuel Duncan, John Billar, Zach. McAulay, Gilbert McRandell, Peter Jenkin, (⁸⁰) Miles Prentice, John Campbel, John Black, John Fisher, Jachelin Smith, (⁸⁵) Michael Smith, John Dilean, John Watts, John Engelke, John Ord, (⁹⁰) Jacob Row, John Hay, Edward Harrison, Murdoch Stewart, James Hanna, (⁹⁵) David Bayne, Will. Brymer, Geo. Hipps, James Rutherford, Robert Jackson, (¹⁰⁰) Robert Wilcocks, Samuel Askwith, Jno. Williams, Charles Winnet, James Isbester, (¹⁰⁵) James Jayring, Ralph Grey, Will. Douglas, Will. Webb, Will. McNabb, (¹¹⁰) Jacob Trader, Joseph Thompson, Richard Dee, John Holman, James Brittan, (¹¹⁵) Philip Mayne, Will. Wright, James McDonald, Henry Goldeys, John Vallence, (¹²⁰) Donald McDonald, John Fraser, John Clark, Will. Osburn, Alexr. McArthur, (¹²⁵) John Ill, John Callahan, Benjamin Walmer, John May, Frans. Sickel, (¹³⁰) — Gilmore, Will. Brown, John Saules, Jacob Stegman, John Sitley, (¹³⁵) Peter Mike, John Miller, William Graham, John Smith, William Brown, (¹⁴⁰) John Platt, Richard Gray, Samuel Young, William Gum, Thomas Aylwin—144 in all.

I do certify that every Protestant House-Keeper in the District of Quebec is included in this List, and that, to the best of my knowledge, there are not ten Protestant free-holders in the Province, consequently not ten Protestants qualified by the Laws of England to be Jurors.

B   JAMES MURRAY.

The Church of England in Canada.

A List of Protestant House-Keepers in Montreal, October 26, 1764.
Justices of the Peace :(¹) John Fraser, — Friesburg, — Ogilvie, Dundas St. Martin, (⁶) Thomas Jamb, — Livingstone, — Goddard, Frans. Noble Knipe, Thomas Walker.

Householders :—(¹⁰) John McQuesne, John Wells, Matthew Wade, Thomas Brayshay, Joseph Howard, (¹⁵) — Vanderhayden, — Arumstringer, — Patterson, — Todd, — McNeall, (²⁰) James Finlay, Richard Dobie, — Artel, — Holmes, — Morrison, (²⁵) Forest Oaks, Edward Chiem, John Stanhouse, Robert Stanhouse, William McCracken, (³⁰) George Young, — Price, — Howard, Thomas Dumis, Joseph Ferey, (³⁵) John Grant, — Porteus, George Geopper, Richard Crafton, Robert Mackay, — Middleburgh, Ebeneezer Stocker, Thomas Barch, John Crossier, John Thompson, (⁴⁵) Will. Jones, John Black, — Walbron, — White, Alexr. Campbel, James Murray, — McClean, Peter McFarland, — De Lisle, — Simonson, (⁵⁵) C. Dessants, Jacob Jane, — Wall.

I do hereby certify that all the Protestant House-Keepers in the District of Montreal are all in the above list.

JAMES MURRAY.

Oct. 2ʳ, 1764.

These lists are contained in the Canadian Archives, Series Q., Vol. 2, pages 332-5.

The result of this attack on Murray's administration was, as any one might conjecture, a compromise. The Grand Jury was greatly blamed by the "King in Council" for its assumptions, even supporting their presentment by the names of French Canadian inhabitants, who had declared that they were fraudulently induced to sign it. And Murray was commanded to signify His Majesty's highest disapprobation of the proceedings of the Grand Jury, and to assure the people "that His Majesty will give the utmost attention and consideration to proper representations from his Canadian subjects, and will cause to be removed every grievance of which they may have reason justly to complain."* At the same time the Government determined to bring a strong influence to bear upon the religion of the new subjects. They must become Protestants. The immense power the French priests wielded over their bodies and souls seemed to leave no other alternative. A similar attempt

---

*Conway to Murray, Can. Arch., Series Q, page 425.

had already been successful in Nova Scotia, and the remarkable work of Dr. Ogilvie in establishing French congregations at Quebec appeared to point out the way in which this work could be done.

Amongst the charges brought against General Murray and his administration, he was accused of "enacting vexatious, oppressive, and unconstitutional ordinances, injurious to civil liberty and the Protestant cause; of discountenancing the Protestant religion by neglecting to attend church; and of failing to provide the Protestants with a place of worship."

General Murray appears before us in his dealing with the people of Canada as an upright, conscientious man, who had the courage of his convictions, and acted upon them. As a churchman, he was loyal to the best traditions of his day, and had a natural repugnance to the common spectacle of sacred things trailing in the mire. The following notice will be read with interest. In the *Quebec Gazette* of the issue of the 20th of December, 1764, is an Ordinance signed by General Murray "for the better observance of keeping the Lord's Day":—

"All keepers of public houses at Quebec, Montreal and Three Rivers shall keep their doors shut during the Time of Divine Service. Everyone over twelve years of age, who shall absent himself from Public Worship of the —— Church for three months shall be fined five shillings."

On the eve of his departure for England, it is recorded that he presented some Church plate and furniture "to the Episcopal Church of the Parish of Quebec."*

General Murray severed his connection with the Government of Canada in the summer of 1766, and, passing over the brief administration of Mr. Irving, he was succeeded by Sir Guy Carleton, who had seen, like himself, gallant service during the conquest of the country.

---
* Canadian Archives, Series Q., Vol. 3, page 205.

CHAPTER III.

THE THREE FRENCH CLERGYMEN.

1766-1800.

WE have now to consider the manner in which the Government carried out the proposals for evangelizing the new subjects—a measure deemed expedient on political grounds only, as no one can charge the Government of the day with entertaining any special anxiety as to their spiritual condition. Dreading the power of the priests, a willing ear was lent to the exaggerated accounts of the Canadian mission field so ripe for the Protestant sickle.*

"The next three clergymen," writes Hawkins, "of whom we find any mention, seem to have been appointed by the Government, under the expectation that an impression might be made upon the French Canadians, by clergymen who could perform the Anglican service in the French language."†

The first of these clergymen was the Rev. David Chadbrand Delisle, a Swiss by birth. As his parish register begins with the 5th of October, 1766, his commission was issued probably by Mr. Irving. At the beginning of his parish register stands the note:—

"Two clergymen officiated in the town of Montreal for three years before my appointment, viz., the Rev. Mr. Ogilvie and the Rev. Mr. Bennett."

At Montreal, Dr. Ogilvie had been succeeded by Rev. Samuel Bennet as the resident missionary. Writing to the Society, Nov. 19, 1764, he states that there were then "but two protestant clergymen, himself included, in Canada," and he complains bitterly that "this unhappy neglect of the mother country to form a religious establishment, was so improved by the Friars and Jesuits as to induce the French inhabitants to look upon their conquerors in an odious light, and to become more impatient of the English yoke." In this letter, Mr. Bennet says that Montreal where "he was accidentally stationed that winter by order of General Gage, was a large city inhabited by nearly one hundred British families, besides many French Protestants... also a garrison containing two Regiments of

---
* Canadian Archives, Series Q., Vol. 49, page 343.
† Annals of the Diocese of Quebec, page 14.

soldiers, who frequently married with French women, and for want of Protestant Clergymen, were obliged to have recourse to Romish Priests to baptize their children." He also declares his intention to return to England with his Regiment unless the Society should appoint him a salary.* The Government, however was determined to appoint French clergymen to the three Canadian Parishes, and Messrs Brooke, Ogilvie and Bennet were recalled—a movement which Colonel Claus subsequently declared, had " been a fatal measure." †

In 1767, we find Mr. Delisle writing to the S. P. G. on the sad and neglected state of the Church of England about Montreal. He stated that the Roman Catholic priests availed themselves greatly of the neglected state of the Church of England in Canada, and persuaded the people that the English had not religion so much at heart as they had, and alleging this neglect as proof of their assertion. At that period he was obliged to officiate, he writes, in the Hospital Chapel, as the English residents were destitute of a place of worship. During the year he had baptized 58 children, a negro boy, an Indian child, and " married 22 couple." ‡

At Quebec, no change appears to have taken place since the departure of Dr. Ogilvie. Chaplains of regiments came and went, Dr. Brooke alone remained. The *Gazette* of the 21st of March, 1765, contains an interesting item concerning him :—

"Sunday last, being the Feast of St. Patrick, the Tutelar of Ireland, the Chief Justice of the Province, with other Civil and Military Officers, Gentlemen and Merchants of that Ancient and Loyal Kingdom, attended Divine Service at the Recollet's Church, when a Sermon suitable to the Day, on the Duty of Praise and Thanksgiving for national Benefits and Blessings, was preached by the Rev. Doctor Brooke, Chaplain to the Garrison, from Isaiah xlii. 12 : *Let them give glory unto the Lord, and declare his Praise in the Islands.* From Church they proceeded to the Sun-Tavern, where an entertainment was prepared for them ; after which many Loyal and Patriotic Toasts were drank : And on Monday Evening they gave a ball, with a cold Collation, to all the Gentlemen and Ladies of the Place at Concert Hall ; and the whole was carried on,

* S. P. G. Record, p. 138.
† S. P. G. Record, p. 139.
‡ S. P. G. Records, p. 139.

and concluded at both Places, with becoming Cheerfulness, perfect Harmony and Decorum."

In the issue of the 21st of May, 1767, is an announcement of the Sunday Services for the coming Summer :—

"On Sunday next, Divine Service according to the Use of the Church of England will be [held] at the Recollet Church, and continue for the Summer Season, beginning soon after eleven : The Drum will beat each Sunday, soon after Half an Hour past Ten, and the Recollet's Bell will ring, to give Notice of the English Service, the Instant their own is ended."

In the issue of the 25th of June, 1767, a Benedick contrasts Marriage with Celibacy from an economical standpoint,—a stupid letter, but the writer incidentally mentions the fact that he pays forty shillings a year for his seat in church.

During the summer, Dr. Brooke's connection with the parish of Quebec came to an end. One of his letters has been given in full; another, also published in the *Gazette*, of the issue of the 11th of April, 1765, advocates innoculation for small-pox; that of the 18th of Aug., 1766, contains his recommendation of Philip Payne ; that of the 22nd of September has his testimonial to Mr. De Croix, a school master; that of the 27th of January, 1767, has this item : "On Tuesday Morning last, Daniel Durns, a Deserter from the 28th Regiment, came and surrendered himself to the Rev. Dr. Brooke, Chaplain to the Garrison. He knew nothing of the pardon proclaimed by Gen. Carleton." Dr. Brooke is supposed to have returned to England. The way was now paved for a further supply of Swiss ministers.

"On Tuesday last," we read in the *Gazette* of the 27th Oct., 1766, "The Reverend Mr. Veyssière, who a few Days since left the Order of the Recollets (amongst whom he was known by the Name of Father Emmanuel) and declared himself a Protestant, took the usual oaths of Allegiance to the King, Abjuration of the Power and Supremacy of the Pope, and Abjuration of the Pretender, and subscribed the Declaration against Popery. He appears to have taken this happy Determination from the laudable Motive of Conscience only, after a long and careful Consideration of the Points in Controversy between the Roman and Protestant Professions, and to have stood in reputable esteem amongst those of the former, as well as the few of the latter he has been known to. The Reverend Father Emmanuel Crespel, the present worthy Commissary of the

Order in this Province, was so just as to say of him, after he had declared his Intention: That he was a Man of very good Behaviour, and exact in all his Duties. A Testimony which does equal Honour to the Candour of the Father Commissary, and the Character of Mr. Veyssière."

Legere Jean Baptiste Noël Veyssière we are informed by members of his family, was born in France about the year 1730. The *Répertoire général du Clergé Canadien, par Mgr. Cyprien Tanguay*, (p. 131), contains the following account of him: "VEYSSIERE, LEGER, en religion frère Emmanuel, recollet, ordonné à Québec, le 27 décembre 1755, desservit les paroisses de Saint Michel et de Beaumont, de 1762 à 1766." Having decided to enter the Church of England, he embarked for London late in the autumn of 1767. On the eve of his departure he published the following card of thanks in the *Gazette* of the 8th of October:—

Au Très Révérénd Pere EMMANUEL CRESPEL, Commissaire des RR.PP. Recollets, aux Messieurs les Protestants, et Catholiques Romains, de la ville de Quebec, semblablement aux Habitants des paroisses, savoir, St. Michel, Beau nont, et St. Nicolas.

Mon. Très Révérend Père, Messieurs, et Habitans autre fois mes paroissiens,—

JE vous fais mes très humbles remercimens des bontés, et de toutes les marques d'estime, que vous m'avez donné quelques jours avant mon depart pour l'Angleterre; je vous en aurai une éternelle reconnaissance. J'ai l'honneur d'etre, avec un profond respect.

Mon Très Révérend Père, Messieurs, &c.,
  Votre très humble et très obeissant Serviteur,
    L. J. B. N. VEYSSIERE.

He was armed with strong recommendations from many of the leading residents, for the appointment to the first pastorate of the town of Three Rivers. Succeeding in his mission, Mr. Veyssière received the Bishop of London's Licence on the 26th of December, and returning to Canada the following year, he, in company with the Rev. Mr. De Montmollin, presented their Royal Mandamus to the Governor, requesting his Excellency's Commissions for the Parishes of Quebec and Three Rivers.

The difficulties Mr. Veyssière and his confrere, Mr. Montmollin, were destined to meet in the way of obtaining their commissions, will be seen in Sir Guy Carleton's letter to the Earl of Hillsborough:—

QUEBEC, 21st July, 1768.

MY LORD,—

I have lately been to visit the Southwest parts of the Province up the Cataraqui, a little beyond our limits, and about forty Leagues up the Great River of the Ottawas; this journey retarded my acknowledging the Receipt of your Lordship's Letters Nos. 1, 2, 3, 4, 5, and 6, they came all safe to Hand, and shall be carefully attended to.

On my return from Montreal, a Mandamus was presented by a Mr. Montmolin, and another by a Mr. Veyssière, formerly a Recollet, directing me to admit and collate, the one to the Church and Parish of Quebec, the other to the Church and Parish of Trois Rivières, to enjoy the same during life, *with all Rights, dues, profits, and Privileges as thereunto belonging, in as full and ample manner as the Ministers of Churches in any of our Colonies in America have usually held and enjoyed, or of Right, ought to hold and enjoy the same.*

As I find these words in every Mandamus, I look upon it as a stile of office that has been adopted for many years for other Provinces, and, under that sanction, unnoticed, has slipped into those for this Province, though under very different circumstances.

These general and extensive expressions have occasioned no small Difficulty already in civil matters, and been the cause of many complaints, giving authority to claim Fees of office, &c., that are Burthensome; but if they be extended to ecclesiastical Property, to dispossess the People of their Parish Churches, and their Clergy of their tithes and all parochial dues, for our Lawyers are clear these words import no less, the evils must be much worse.

As I judge it impossible this could have been designed, and that your Lordship could not have failed to communicate to me if a measure of such consequence had been resolved upon, I have in the meanwhile, and till I am certain of the King's pleasure therein, granted them Commissions which leave them power to do all the good they can, or chuse to do, without authorizing them to do mischief.

I had so mean an opinion of Mr. Veyssière that I refused to recommend him, when he went to Europe last year, and had I not imagined my silence of a Person leaving the Province, notwithstanding his letters of recommendation from others, which anyone may procure, would have prevented his return with the King's

Mandamus, I should have thought myself obliged to have given a full account of his levity and folly, both before and after his renouncing the errors of the Church of Rome.

Mr. Montmoulin, notwithstanding we have in this town the use of two Churches in common with the Roman Catholics, and one entirely to ourselves,* thinks it very hard the Parish Church, which we took for a store, on our arrival, having no further occasion for it, nor money to preserve it from Ruin, it was given up to them above a year ago, and it is now almost repaired at a considerable expense. He thinks it still harder I disapprove of his taking the Tithes; I endeavoured to show him the Violence, Injustice, and Breach of Treaties with Protestants; he, therefore, sees no reason why we should keep ours with Roman Catholics.

In our present situation, we have more Church room, in common with the Roman Catholics, than we want, and if the order which prohibits the Recollets and Jesuits from recruiting their converts is continued, we shall, in a few years, without violence, or giving offence, and without appearing to depart from the general Lenity of the King's judgment, have more churches to ourselves than we can possibly occupy or keep in Repair, unless the Treasurer is pleased to assist us with money for that purpose. A copy of their commission is herewith inclosed.

> I am, with much Respect and Esteem,
> Your Lordship's
> Most obedient, Humble Servant,
> GUY CARLETON.

The Earl of Hillsborough,
 One of His Majesty's principal
 Secretary of State, &c., &c.

The quotation from the Royal Mandamus, contained in this letter, is important. Doubtless the form used in issuing these documents exists in the Colonial Office and elsewhere; but I have not been able to see a copy, and I doubt if many people in Canada are familiar with the paper. The same may be said of the clerical commissions issued by the Governors. For this reason I shall offer no apology for printing here the special commission granted by Sir Guy Carleton to Messrs. De Montmollin and Veyssière, referred to

---

* Presbyterian services were held in the chapel of the Jesuits, but the statement that we had one church entirely to ourselves is inexplicable.

n the above letter, and which admitted them to the pastorate of the Parishes of Quebec and Three Rivers, posts held by them till the end of the century.*

To the HONOURABLE GUY CARLETON, Lieutenant-Governor and Commander-in-Chief of the Province of Quebec, Brigadier General of His Majesty's Forces, etc.

To.................Clerk. Greeting:

In obedience to His Majesty's commands, signified by his Mandamus, dated at St. James', the 12th day of February last, I do admit you to be Curate and Minister of the Gospel in the Parish of [Quebec] in the Province of Quebec, to perform the office of a Curate and Minister of the Gospel in such Church or place set apart for the performance of Divine Service as is or shall hereafter be appointed by the Governor or Commander-in-Chief of this Province, in reading the Common Prayers and performing the other services of the Church belonging to the office of a Priest, according to the Form set forth in the Book of Common Prayer and Administration of the Sacraments according to the Use of the Church of England, and not otherwise, or in any other manner, you having first sworn, in some of His Majesty's Courts of Record in this Province, on the Holy Evangelists to renounce all foreign jurisdiction and to bear Faith and true Allegiance to His Majesty, King George the 3d, according to an Act of Parliament in that case made and provided, and to pay true and Canonical obedience to the Lord Bishop of London and his successors, Bishops of London, [to] Hold and enjoy the said office of Curate and Minister of the Gospel, together with all such dues as shall arise from Persons professing the Protestant Religion according to the Reformation of the Church of England, and not otherwise.

Given.....................21st July, 1768.

The answer of the Secretary of the Colonies to Carleton's letter is to the effect that the form of commission issued to the two clergymen is approved, that the support of the Church of England and the toleration of the new subjects in the exercise of the Roman Catholic religion will be matters of serious attention in the general regulations, that protection is to be given to the Established Church, and that care is to be taken that its offices are conducted with decency.

---

*These documents are contained in the Canadian Archives, Series Q, Vol. 52, pages 726-730.

The Secretary expresses much concern that the appointment of Mr. Veyssière is not agreeable to the Governor's wishes. He has communicated with the Bishop of London on the subject, and now encloses a copy of the Bishop's letter concerning the matter. In his rejoinder, the Bishop writes that if a mistake has been made, it is through the Governor's own fault. Had Sir Guy Carleton sent his objection before Mr. Veyssière's return to Canada, he would not have solicited his appointment; but he had sent no objections, and the recommendations produced were so strong that he had no option in the matter.*

The expectations of the zealous memorialists were bitterly disappointed in the result of their labours. The French Canadians were not ready for wholesale conversion, and, to make matters worse, these French clergy, through their imperfect apprehension of the English language, were unable to minister intelligibly to their parishioners. Complaints of inefficiency began to pour in, and year after year, the *Reports on the State of Religion* spoke bitterly of the unsatisfactory condition of the Church of England throughout the country. Indeed, these complaints became the order of the day ; but the Government refused to notice them. It will be more convenient to consider these complaints in a future chapter.

Beyond the particulars given on a former page concerning the appointment of the Rev. Mr. Delisle to Montreal, I have few details of his life and labours, excepting the evidence provided by the Parish registers kept by him, and which are in the custody of the Rector of Christ Church Cathedral. From these we learn that he was married, and left several children at his death.

Francis De Montmollin was born at New Chatel, Switzerland. He was a son of the Count De Montmollin, and, therefore, a member of the Bourbon family. His brother John is frequently mentioned in General Haldimand's Diary. One of his sisters was a maid of honour to Queen Charlotte. Mr. De Montmollin married an English lady, Jane Bell, in London. Coming to Canada in 1768 as Minister of Quebec, and continuing at his post during the restless years of the American revolution, his pastorate was necessarily an eventful one. †

---

* Canadian Archives, Series Q, Vol. 5-2, pp. 756-8.

† I am indebted to Mrs. Dorion, of Drummondville, a grand-daughter of Mr. De Montmollin for these particulars.

Throughout his pastorate services were conducted at the Recollet's Church. A picture of the interior of this church may be seen at the rooms of the Quebec Literary and Historical Society. The church stood on a site a little to the east of the English Cathedral.

"Although the British settlers at Quebec had obtained a clergyman," writes Hawkins, "they had no church. They did not scruple, therefore, to apply to the Order of the Recollets to allow them the use of their chapel during those hours on the Sunday when it was not required for their own service This request was at once most generously complied with; and the first regular church-services in Canada were thus performed in a chapel belonging to a Franciscan Order of the Church of Rome. After every English service, the chapel was subjected to a regular lustration for the removal of the pollution which it was thus supposed to have contracted."*

As there is considerable uncertainty in many quarters as to the burial places of the British residents of Quebec for many years after the Conquest, it will not be amiss to examine the subject here.

Mr. Le Moine writes: "It was only in the spring of 1657 that the new cemetery called St. Joseph's Cemetery, adjoining the Roman Catholic Cathedral, and between it and the Seminary, was used for the first time.........This St. Joseph's Cemetery was used until the Conquest, by Roman Catholics exclusively; after the surrender of Quebec, we find in the old *Quebec Gazette* obituary notices, according to which the remains of Protestants seem to have been committed to the St. Joseph's Cemetery."†

Mr. Le Moine probably refers to the following interesting notices.

"On the 12th of the month died here, in the 34th year of his age, Mr. Joseph Senilk, merchant; he was born at Cosade, near Aux, the Capital of Gascony, but he had resided some years past in this Province. *He is the first Protestant we have lost since the Conquest of the Place, and the only one that ever was admitted in it to the Rites of Christian Burial.*"

"And on Friday, the 24th, died also, of a Flux, attended at the last with a Fever, Mr. Mark Anderson, Merchant, Partner of Mr. George Fulton.........Both these Gentlemen were men of probity, worth and piety.........They were both buried with decent funeral honours in the Church-yard of the Cathedral, on the North side, the former on the 13th and the latter on the 25th."

---

* Annals of the Diocese of Quebec, page 14.
† Quebec, Past and Present, page 440.

These obituary notices are in the *Gazette* of the 30th of August, 1764. Several similar notices are subsequently made mentioning the same place of burial.

In the issue of the 16th of April, 1767, however, we find a letter signed "An Englishman," which gives an alarming account of the condition of this cemetery, and the writer begs his countrymen to subscribe a shilling each towards the repair of the wall of the Cathedral Church-yard. The rejoinder to this appeal appeared a fortnight later, signed by "H. Morin, Church Warden, in office for the Parish of this City, for the present year." On account of its importance I reproduce the letter :

To the Printers :—

I have seen in your *Gazette*, No. 120, an observation, and signed *An Englishman*, relative to a *pre'ended Burying Ground, lying behind* the Parish Church of this City, which he says is in a very bad condition, and his intention would be that the wall that incloses it, part of which is fallen, should be repaired. I think it my duty to inform the author of these reflections, that this pretended burying-ground is a garden, belonging to the parsonage (or priest's house), which was used as such to the time of the siege of Quebec, when the parsonage-house being burnt, together with the church, the said garden was neglected, but not abandoned, and, consequently, it belongs to the managers of the Fabrick Lands, and not to any other persons, to repair the said wall. And, as the opportunity offers, I pray the English gentlemen may no longer use the same as a burying-ground, to the end that the Parish Priest may, whenever he shall think proper, make use of his garden, in the same manner as every individual peaceably enjoys his own Property.

I am truly, GENTLEMEN,

H. MORIN, etc.

We are thus informed by the Warden of the Roman Catholic Parish Church that the English dead were not buried in the St. Joseph's Cemetery, but in a garden back of the Cathedral. Instead of resting in St. Joseph's Cemetery, General Murray records a somewhat different treatment. " He, Montgolfier," Murray writes, " pushed matters so far as to have the dead bodies of some soldiers taken up, because Heretics should not be interred in consecrated ground. Such behaviour could not fail of giving great disgust to the King's British Subjects in these parts. If so haughty and imperious a priest, well related in France, is placed at the Head of the Church in this Country, he may hereafter occasion much mischief if ever he finds a proper opportunity to display his rancour and malice."*

In a letter of the issue of the 21st of January, 1768, we read :— If we had a P-t-st-t C-h we should of course have a B-ry-ng Groun l, in which case a P—t–st—t's B–dy would have some chance of rest in the g–ave, as the C—d—ns would probably find ground enough in Canada to build upon, without finding it needful of raising P—t–st—t's B–d—s in order to lay the foundations of their buildings." This letter seems to refer to the garden already mentioned.

Not long after the date of these letters, the old "Protestant Cemetery" in St. John Street, and the gorge of the St. Louis Gate Bastion, were opened as special Protestant Cemeteries.

Mr. Veyssière's connection with the Parish of Three Rivers is thus recorded at the beginning of his Register :

"Registre. Contenant les actes de Baptêmes, Marriages, et Sepultres, de l'Eglise protestante de la ville de Trois Rivières en Canada, et de la garrison.

—1768—

"Le premier pasteur en a été le Reverend M. Legère Jean Baptiste Noël Veyssiere, en l'anné 1767, 26th Decembre, et il le a pris possession le 25th Septembre le 12th Dimanche apres la Trinité de l'année 1768. Et c'est à la plus grande gloire de dieu que je me destine, et a l'edification de son cher tropeau."

This Register is written in French throughout.

On the 17th of April, 1770, Mr. Veyssière married Mrs. Elizabeth Brookes at Quebec, the witnesses being the Rev. James Montgomery, chaplain of the 10th Regiment, and George Dame. The two daughters of this lady, Mary and Jane Chease, were already married, respectively to Ensign George Dame, of the 8th Regiment, whose name is given above, and Lieut. Waldro Kelly, of the 10th. A romantic story concerning Mr. Veyssière's marriage is still related by the descendants of Mr. Dame. It is said that Père Emmanuel Crespel, commissary of the Recollet order, confined him to one of the cells in the Convent at Quebec, in the hope that this wholesome discipline would break his infatuation, but that he

---

* Can. Arch., Series Q., Vol. I, pp. 268, 260.

succeeded in communicating his condition to his English friends by means of a scrap of birch-bark, and thus effected a release from his involuntary confinement. But this tradition would seem to be most improbable in the face of Père Crespel's testimony to his good behaviour, and his own card of thanks to his former superior.

Services had been performed in the Recollet Church at Three Rivers since 1762 * by the military chaplains at that post, and they have continued in the same place uninterruptedly to the present day. This church is therefore the oldest Anglican church in Canada.

In speaking of the church buildings at Three Rivers it seems proper to refer to their history. The present rectory was the Recollet monastery, and St. James Church the chapel of the monastery. When the Recollets were permitted to return to Canada in 1670, they set to work at once to build houses for their order at Quebec, Montreal, and Three Rivers. A paper on the condition of the Order in New France, drawn up in 1682, states that they had then a Convent at Three Rivers, but no inmates, as the Bishop had some three years before caused it to be closed.† These buildings are the sole ecclesiastical remains now standing of the earliest missionaries to Canada. ‡ At the Conquest the Recollets abandoned their house at Three Rivers, and the Crown entered into possession. The church was utilized as a court house and a storehouse for hospital effects, a wood partition being built up between them. The monastery became the jail of the District, and the sacristy was used as a sheriff's office. The Government provided a place for religious services by making part of the old church do duty on Sunday as a church, and at all other times as a court house. This arrangement was continued until 1795, when the western part, heretofore used as a store for medicines, was given exclusively for church services.*

The old cemetery at Three Rivers is the ground on which the old powder magazine stands. It is a pity that the Government saw fit, a few years ago, to sell this ground, in which some hundreds of soldiers and civilians were buried.

---
* Les Ursulines des Trois-Rivières, p. 433.
† Histoire Chronologique de la Nouvelle France en Canada, Appendice, p. 217.
‡ Les Ursulines des Trois-Rivières, p. 433.
* S. P. G, Records, p. 143.

CHAPTER IV.

INFLUENCE OF THE AMERICAN WAR.

THE Church in its three centres, under the French ministers, simply stagnated until the passing of the Quebec Act of 1774. There were no other clergymen of the Anglican Church then in Canada except an army chaplain at Quebec.*

Hitherto the French Canadians had had no political or even religious status—for they had been ruled and treated for fifteen years as British subjects, and were rapidly becoming Anglified. But the year 1774 saw the introduction of a Bill into the British House of Parliament, granting them distinct privileges which amounted to nothing less than a distinct nationality. The steps to this enactment were as follows:

Sir Guy Carleton visited England in 1773, and whilst there he was faced by two petitions to the King, one from the British and the other from the French residents of Canada. The former stated that the British residents numbered something over three thousand, and they begged the King to instruct the Governor to convene the House of Assembly, expressly granted to them by the terms of the Royal Proclamation of 1763, and for which they had waited ten long years. They strongly claimed that the situation and circumstances of the Province required the immediate fulfilment of this measure. On the other hand the French petition complained of the inconvenience of English law, and asked for the restoration of their ancient laws, privileges and customs; that Canada should be restored to its former limits; and that the French Canadians should be entitled to all the privileges accorded to British subjects.

This Bill was pushed through the House of Parliament, and received the royal assent with great haste. Some writers see in this action of the Imperial Government only a strong desire to perform a simple act of justice to a long-suffering people, whilst others claim that it was the hasty action of a Government almost panic-stricken at the possibility of a Canadian junction with the American insurgents, and that further privileges still would have been accorded had they been solicited. Into the merits of this question we do not propose to enter.

---

* Memoir of Bishop Mountain, page 383.

The clauses of this Bill which affected the religious status of the residents of Canada are as follows :

" V. And for the more perfect security and ease of the minds of the inhabitants of the said province, it is hereby declared, that his Majesty's subjects, professing the religion of the Church of Rome, of and in the said Province of Quebec, may have, hold, and enjoy the free exercise of the religion of the Church of Rome, subject to the King's supremacy, declared and established by an Act, made in the first year of the reign of Queen Elizabeth, over all the dominions and countries which then did, or thereafter should belong, to the Imperial Crown of this Realm; and that the Clergy of the said Church may hold, receive and enjoy their accustomed dues and rights, with respect to such persons only as shall profess the said Religion.

" VI. Provided, nevertheless, that it shall be lawful for His Majesty, his heirs or successors, to make such provisions out of the rest of the said accustomed dues and rights, for the encouragement of the Protestant Religion, and for the maintenance and support of a Protestant Clergy, within the said province, as he or they shall from time to time think necessary and expedient.

" VIII. And be it further enacted by the authority aforesaid that all his Majesty's Canadian subjects within the Province of Quebec, the religious Orders and Communities only excepted, may also hold and enjoy their property and possessions, together with all customs and usages relative thereto, and all other their civil rights in as large, ample and beneficial manner, as if the said proclamation, commissions, ordinances, and other acts and instruments, had not been made, and as may consist with their allegiance to His Majesty, and the subjection to the Crown and Parliament of Great Britain; and that in all matters of controversy, relative to property and civil rights, resort shall be had to the laws of Canada, as the rule for the decision of the same."

By this celebrated Act, the French Civil Law, and of course the French language, besides the Roman Catholic Hierarchy, were established in the country. Tithes and all other Church dues were now made legally collectable, after they had been for fifteen years in abeyance. Roman Catholic disabilities as to tenure of office were removed. The clergy were permitted to hold real estate. Writers like Gerald Hart claim that by this Bill the whole fabric of English dominion in the Province of Quebec was forever, at one blow, annihilated, leaving merely a British protectorate to mark the result of the heroic conquest of Wolfe and Amherst.*

The immediate effect of the American War of Independence upon the Church of England in Canada was the settlement in the country of some twenty thousand or more Loyalists who were driven out of the revolted provinces. To them the Quebec Act was most distasteful, being characterized as the "Act for the Establishment of Popery in the Province of Quebec," and it was to their repeated and persistent demands that this Act was virtually annulled by the passing of the Constitutional Act of 1791.

The first effect, however, of the American war upon the Anglican Church in Canada was the introduction of the abuse called *non-residence*. As an experiment it was not found conducive to the best interests of the Church, and I cannot find that it was repeated. The Reverend Lewis Guerry was appointed to the "Fourth Parish" in Canada [Sorel], in the year 1774. He came out to Canada during the season, and found the country convulsed, he says, by the American struggle for independence. As the war prevented the settling of his parish, and his services were declined by Mr. De Montmollin, and presumably by the pastors at Montreal and Three Rivers, Mr. Guerry remained a year at Quebec, after which he obtained the Governor's permission to return to England. For ten years he continued to reside in the old country, receiving from the Government £200 per annum as the holder of a Canadian benefice. At the expiration of that period, he was permitted to exchange his benefice with Mr. Toosey. As he did not return to Canada, it is unnecessary to follow Mr. Guerry's career more fully, except to print the Earl of Plymouth's letter concerning him and his case, as a specimen of the manner in which his leave of absence was procured from year to year.

HOWELL, BROWNSGROVE,

Worcestershire, Feb. 11, 1783.

SIR :—I beg leave to trespass upon your time in behalf of the Rev. Mr. Guerry, whose case is contained in the enclosed. I undertook to trouble Lord Grantham sometime back on the same occasion, from a mistake, who informed me of my error, and that he had sent Mr. Guerry's and my Letters to you. If there is no impropriety

---

* Quebec Act of 1774, by Gerald E. Hart, page 12.

or fresh obstacle, I trust you will excuse the freedom I now take in requesting you to consider of my application and to grant it, as I must acknowledge myself interested in endeavouring to keep in my neighbourhood a gentleman of sense and character. I have the honour to subscribe myself with great Regard, Sir,

Your most obedient Humble Servant,
PLYMOUTH.

The following paper was enclosed in the letter. They are contained in the Canadian Archives, Series Q, Vol. 21, pp. 64-6.

"*A true state of the Rev. Mr. Lewis Guerry's case as the last appointed minister of the Church of England, in the Province of Quebec, according to what can be shown to be matters of fact.*

"The said Lewis Guerry Repaired to that Province with the first ships that sailed, after his appointment, and found what was yet unknown in England, the said Province invaded by the Americans, which having prevented the settling of the fourth parish he was appointed to (as the continuation of the American war has ever since untill now), left him, as the then Governor General, Sir Guy Carleton, can witness, nothing to do but to assist of his own good will the present Rector of Quebec, who, it is well known at that place, seemed far from wishing for assistance, and declared he wanted it not. The two other parishes, Three Rivers and Montreal were likewise provided for. So that on these considerations, after having remained there above twelve-month, the Governor, after the Siege of Quebec was raised, readily granted the said Lewis Guerry leave to come over to England for twelve-month, as long a time, his Excellency added, as he had it in his power to grant, and upon the same considerations, a continuation of the same Leave of absence has been to this day yearly granted to the said Lewis Guerry without difficulty by the Secretary of State in London, applied to for that purpose. And the said Lewis Guerry can make it plainly appear that the present Governor of Quebec thinks not his presence in that Province necessary, until a change in the present state of affairs (against which, not knowing how soon it may take place, he holds him in readiness to perform his duty) occasions the fixing and settling of the place he was appointed to, without which his residence in the said Province of Quebec still remains perfectly unnecessary, whilst his continuing in the mean season in England is very essential to the good of his affairs, which he will otherwise ever be found ready to give up, the moment his Duty calls upon him. But humbly hopes until *then*, and as long as matters remain in the situation that has been stated, as they now still do, and as he does not expect they will much longer, his present Request of a renewal of his Leave of absence will be graciously condescended to."

It is somewhat remarkable that the next clergyman who officiated at Sorel should also meet with insurmountable difficulties in the way of ministering to the people of that place. But here the coincidence ends, as he was bodily on the spot, and most anxious to serve the post. Possibly Mr. Guerry's leave of absence may have been the cause of the Governor's reluctance to the appointment.

It is a thousand pities that we must chronicle a very unseemly and unedifying proceeding, but as we have undertaken to record the facts that have come to our knowledge concerning the struggles of the Church in her early days in Canada, this blot cannot be allowed to pass unnoticed. Briefly stated, Mr. Scott quarrelled with the military authorities, into which the gentle General Riedesel and the Governor of the Province were drawn, before the matter was laid before the Bishop of London, and eventually settled by him.

Thomas Charles Heslop Scott had held the post of deputy chaplain to the 34th Regiment. The earliest notice I have seen of him is contained in the *Quebec Gazette* of the 15th of July, 1779 :

" On Saturday evening, the 3rd inst., was married at Sorel, by the Rev. Mr. Scott, Mr. George Ross, merchant, to Miss Isabella McDonell, niece of Captain McDonell, an amiable young lady, possessed of every qualification to make that very honourable state truly happy."

The cause of the rupture was the order for disbanding the regiment. Col. St. Leger, commandant at Sorel, notified Scott of the order, whereupon the chaplain responded in a characteristic letter in which the colonel was directly charged with rank cowardice, brutality, etc., and informed that he refused to accept dismissal at his hands. He then wrote to the Governor, General Haldimand, complaining of Colonel St. Leger's treatment, and asking for redress.*

---

* Canadian Archives, Haldimand Collection, Series B, Vol. 74, page 181.

Towards the end of December, 1779, a petition was drawn up and numerously signed, purporting to come from the inhabitants of Sorel, and praying that Mr. Scott be appointed by the Governor as minister of the parish. This document being received at headquarters, General Haldimand took the practical, if somewhat original, plan of issuing orders to General Riedesel, to ascertain the character of each signer of the petition, and to set it opposite its corresponding signature in the petition.* At the beginning of January, General Riedesel reported that he had investigated the character of the subscribers to the paper, with the result that all the signers without exception were "suttlers." He reported Scott a turbulent and dangerous fellow, and begged permission to send him away from Sorel where he had nothing to do.† The Governor replied that he viewed with alarm the proposal to turn such a man as Scott loose on Montreal or Quebec, where he could do so much harm. It were better to leave him at Sorel until he can be sent out of the country altogether.‡ General Riedesel then hit upon a plan of settling the difficulty, by requiring all the signers to withdraw their signatures from the document. This would cut the ground from under the chaplain's feet completely Captain Barnes of the Royal Artillery was entrusted with the execution of this delicate task. At the same time Scott was commanded to stop preaching. He was sure, Riedesel wrote to the Governor, that he was in for a good round of abuse from Scott, as Colonel St. Leger had already been before him, but he should pay no attention to anything he should say or do.§ But Captain Barnes did not find his task an easy one. Before he had well begun, Scott encountered him, with the result that he was very roughly handled by the matter-of-fact soldier. Whereupon he complained bitterly to the Governor of this "hostile and unprovoked attack," adding that the stoppage of the religious services had led to the establishment of Sunday recreations, "to the detriment" of the people.‖

Scott's next movement was the distribution of some extraordinary hand-bills,** a proceeding which the Governor met by recommend-

---

* Can. Arch., Hald. Col., Series B, Vol. 13, page 89.
† Do., Vol. 137, page 1.
‡ Do., Vol. 139, page 97.
§ Do., Vol. 137, page 7.
‖ Do., Vol. 74, page 373.
** Do., Vol. 137, page 246.

ing all to ignore. "The greatest punishment," he wrote, " a fellow like Scott can feel, will be to ignore his hand-bills." At the same time he assured General Riedesel " that he would institute inquiries, and as soon as sufficient proof was adduced against him, he would send the ex-chaplain out of the Province.*" In the meantime, Scott began legal proceedings against Captain Barnes, in view of which General Riedesel assured the Governor that the Captain had only acted under orders, and he suggested the propriety of laying the matter before the Attorney General,† a course which was followed immediately.‡

Without pursuing minutely this extraordinary case, it is sufficient to say that many wearying letters followed in the same strain, until July, 1784, a year later, when, at the Governor's recommendation, Col. St. Leger transmitted to Lord Frederick Cavendish the eviden· of the presumption and unworthy conduct of Scott in the Province of Quebec. This action caused a reference to be made to the Bishop of London, who advised Scott to submit to the Governor, a course presumably followed, as there is a letter of his to the Governor offering to put himself entirely into his Excellency's hands.

There is a tradition at Sorel which was transmitted by Rev. Mr. Jackson to Canon Anderson, that Scott was considered a very able man, and an eloquent preacher.

His letter of the 5th of October, 1784, is here reproduced as containing references to his life, which the reader may find interesting. It is in the Haldimand Collection, vol. 2, p. 194.

SIR—

I had the honour last post to receive a letter from the Lord Bishop of London, wherein I find his Lordship had been as much imposed upon as your Excellency and Major General de Riedesel relative to me. I have the happiness to acquaint your Excellency that it was late in June before the deception was found out. As I was not upon his Lordship's list nor his worthy predecessors as a licensed preacher, it never was supposed that any regular, ordained clergyman would have submitted to have accepted of a Deputy Chaplainship. I never supposed that Mr. St. Leger could have

---
* Can. Arch., Hald. Col., Series B, Vol. 139, page 195.
† Do., Vol. 138, page 260.
‡ Do., Vol. 139, page 333.

lost sight of honour, without acquainting me, as I would have readily convinced him of my ordination, though, when I reflect, I have repeatedly been insulted by his superscriptions. The late Lord Bishop of London recommended me to your Excellency's predecessor, Sir Guy Carleton, and I suppose his Lordship would not have recommended me had I not been a proper person. I was twice taken by the Rebels, and lost everything of value I was possessed of. I suppose, if any officer in His Majesty's service had been taken by the said Privateer, he would have lost every part of his baggage, and provided his commission had been packed up with his Baggage, his commission also. Nevertheless his Rank and Pay would be just the same. Upon my being carried into Halifax from the French Island, St. Peter, the Bishop of London's Commissary whom I had known in England, desired me to do duty, which I did all the Sundays I remained in Halifax. Your Excellency's humanity is well known, and I flatter myself that my extream distress will not make your Excellency think any proposition from me too presumptuous. I am ready and willing to withdraw my civil and my criminal actions against Barnes & Co., for the injuries done me, upon Captain Barnes or any one for him paying me the exact sum which I have suffered, being £300 subscription, £21.15.0, Law expences in Canada. I likewise will withdraw my impeachment against the Court, which is drawn up by my council's desire, and these transactions shall forever be buried in oblivion. Upon my receiving your Excellency's gracious answer, I am to propose to Brigadier St. Leger the purchase of the copyright of the correspondence between us for £210, which sum is by no means equal in any proportion for the pain and anguish I have laboured under for years, having incurred your Excellency's displeasure by Mr. St. Leger only. There being in Canada (only) 238 copies subscribed for. If your Excellency should not be graciously pleased to accede to the above terms, I hope your Excellency will put it in my power to discharge my Debts and to go home. If your Excellency approves of my Terms, I am to remain in Canada till your Excellency's successor arrives, and if his Excellency would not be graciously pleased to employ or appoint me, I shall leave the Province next Spring. I have taken the liberty to enclose to your Excellency the Lord Bishop's superscription, and should the contents—but honour forbids it in every sense. Do not, Gracious Sir, think me too presumptuous in soliciting your Excellency's answer as soon as possible, when I assure your Excellency, you have not in Canada a more faithful servant than him who has the honour to subscribe himself with the highest sense of Duty and Respect,

Sir, Your Excellency's Most faithful Humble Servant,
Thomas Charles Heslop Scott.

Sorel, 5th October, 1784.

His Excellency,
    General Haldimand.

Subsequently Mr. Scott retired to Quebec where he opened a private school.* Here he died on the 21st of March, 1813.†

---

* Canon Anderson is my authority for this statement.
† Cathedral Register.

CHAPTER V.

THE THREE LOYALIST CLERGYMEN.

THE first clergyman of the United-Empire-Loyalist stock was the Rev. Dr. John Doty, a man whose name was well known a century ago, and left its mark in indelible characters stamped into the religious and political life of the American colonies both before and during the period of the Revolutionary war.

He was born in New York city on the 8th of May, 1745.* He was the eldest of four or five children of Jabez Doty, and a direct descendant of Edward Doty, one of the Pilgrim Fathers who landed at Plymouth Rock from the Mayflower in 1620. His mother's name was Mary Price. She was a daughter of John Price, a Lieutenant in the Queen's Fusiliers. John Doty's father, as we would suppose, was a Puritan of the strictest kind, but his mother was a churchwoman. She not only brought him considerable private means, and good family connections, but also a conservative tendency in politics and religion ; and he acquired at an early age a strong desire for culture, position, and influence.

In 1768 he entered King's (now Columbia) College, New York. He graduated in 1770, and was married the same year to Lydia Burling. During the summer he officiated as a lay reader, and in the autumn sailed for England. He was admitted to Deacon's Orders, the 23rd of October, in the Chapel Royal, Westminster, ordained Priest in the same church, the 1st of January, 1771, by the Bishop of Norwich, and duly licenced to officiate in the Province of New York.

Returning to America, he was appointed Rector of the Parish of St. Peter's, Peekskill, Westchester County, New York, where he was inducted on the 16th of July, 1771. Two years later he resigned this living, and was appointed to the charge of Schenectady, at the earnest solicitation of the Vestry of the Church, and especially of the Rev. William Andrews, his predecessor, who thus spoke of him to Sir William Johnson, in a letter of the 16th of August, 1773:
" This gentleman who now officiates in my room is personally known to Colonel Johnson, and I believe would, if agreeable to you and the

---

* I am indebted to Ethan Allen Doty, Esq., of New York, for the personal items in this sketch.

people, accept the Mission. He is a relative of Ellice's, a person of good abilities, and a fair character." He remained at Schenectady till 1775, when, on the outbreak of the American War of Independence, he became an object of suspicion on account of his strong sympathy with the mother country, and his well-known antipathy to the views of the revolutionists. Divine service was suspended in his church, he was himself harshly treated on several occasion, annoyed by repeated arrests, and finally on Whit-Monday, 1777, he was taken into custody by the insurgents for his unswerving loyalty to his King and country. Seeing nothing before him but imprisonment for an indefinite period, he now deemed it prudent to apply for liberty to remove to Canada, and in due time he received notice that he was free to leave the country.

On the 23rd of October, 1777, Mr. Doty left the Province of New York for Canada, and the means for travelling were so imperfect at that period that he did not arrive at Montreal until the 17th of the following month. Here he was at once appointed to the chaplaincy of His Majesty's Royal Regiment of New York, the 60th.

As the subsequent movements of Dr. Doty are of historical value as well as of ecclesiastical interest, the reader will pardon me if I seem to bestow too much attention to the various events of his Canadian career. In the month of June, 1778, he accompanied his regiment to Quebec, and in August visited Sorel for the first time. Not long afterwards, General Haldimand acquainted Sir John Johnson with the fact that a memorial had been presented by the inhabitants of Montreal requesting the appointment of the Rev. John Doty, the chaplain, to the management of a public school in Montreal, and that, if Sir John approved, there was no objection to the appointment.*

This appointment, however, was not made, and Dr. Doty soon afterwards made arrangements to go to England, being allowed the privilege of retaining his chaplaincy during his absence. On the 23rd of October, 1781, accompanied by Mrs. Doty, he embarked for England on board the ship *Integrity*, in company of a "convoy of 60 sail." Arriving at London on the 4th of January, 1782, he spent the winter in England, but the following spring was obliged to return to Canada to obtain an extension of his leave of absence.

---

* Canadian Archives, Haldimand Collection, Letters to Officers of the King's Royal Reg. of N. Y., Series B, Vol. 158, page 125, 23rd Nov., 1780.

The Three Loyalist Clergymen.   47

Hoping for success he left Mrs. Doty in England. Hitherto his Canadian duty during his absence had been supplied by his fellow-loyalist, Rev. John Stuart, who now strongly supported Mr. Doty's application, as an extended leave of absence, he wrote to General Haldimand, would, through the receipt of Mr. Doty's half pay, prove an acceptable addition to his income.*

Succeeding in his application, Mr. Doty again went to England, landing at Plymouth on the 26th of November, 1782. Then came the Declaration of Peace, and finding it difficult to provide a subtitute for his duty in Canada, he was glad to accept the appointment of Minister of Sorel. Leaving London in April, 1783, he arrived at Quebec on the 13th of June, by the ship *Ranger*, and at once made preparations for entering upon his new duties as the first resident pastor of Sorel.

Dr. Doty arrived at Sorel on the 1st of July, 1784, having met with difficulties which effectually prevented an earlier accomplishment of his wishes. There is a letter in the Haldimand Collection, written the day of his arrival, asking from the Governor for a residence, provisions, and a lot of land,† and another from Captain Barnes to Matthews stating that Mr. Doty had arrived, and that quarters had been assigned him in the barracks until orders should be received from headquarters.

On the 4th of July, 1784, Dr. Doty celebrated divine service for the first time at Sorel.‡ As in the three older parishes, the earliest services here were held in the Roman Catholic church. But after four weeks, permission to use the parish church was withdrawn, and Dr. Doty applied to Major Matthews, on the 4th of August, for the use of a government building for religious services.

"The first church in which he ministered," wrote Canon Anderson, in his sermon preached at the Centennial celebration of Christ Church, Sorel, " was of wood, and it was originally a marine store, fitted up for divine service in something of church-like form, with belfry and bell, the self-same bell which now hangs in our spire. This church was situated near the present market-house and barrack yard. A government survey of the town, however, having thrown this building into one of the principal streets, it was ordered

---
* Can. Arch., Haldimand Collection, Series B, Vol. 158, page 275, Aug. 28, 1782.
† Do , Vol. 162, page 321.
‡ Diary of Rev. John Doty.

to be removed; and the Rector and Congregation, selling the old building to the best advantage, proceeded forthwith to the erection of a new church, on a better site, granted to them by the Government, upon the Royal Square." In his reports to the S. P. G., Dr. Doty states that when the Roman church was no longer available, he obtained permission to "fit up a barrack" in which a congregation of 150 assembled "every Lord's Day." In 1785, he purchased "one of the best houses in Sorel, part of a bankrupt's effects, for only 15 guineas, out of a collection of over £30 which he had obtained in Montreal." It was fitted for a church, so as to accommodate above 120 persons, and opened for service on Christmas Day, 1785, when it was crowded, and 32 persons received the Communion. Soon after, Brigadier General Hope, Lieutenant-Governor and Commander in Chief, gave five guineas, Captain Barnes of the Royal Artillery, a bell, and Captain Gother Man, "some boards and timber." This encouraged them to add a steeple to their church which was finished about mid-summer. "Such was the erection of the first English church in old Canada."[*] His diary contains the following entry under the date, Christmas, 1785: "Completed the first Protestant church built in Canada, and opened it for Divine Service." By the aid of Lord Dorchester, the present church was erected, and opened for service on the 3d of October 1790.[†]

At the beginning of his pastorate at Sorel, Dr. Doty reported to the S. P. G. that the mission contained about seventy Protestant families, made up of various denominations, but all of whom attended the services of the Church. The total number of communicants was twenty-nine. Two years later they had increased to fifty.

The following summer he received an invitation to become the pastor of St. Peter's Church, Albany, but having visited that part of the country, he returned again to Sorel. His stipend of £50 per annum was paid by the S. P. G. In 1786, Dr. Maurice requested the Government to make him an allowance also. This was done, his name appearing in subsequent lists as receiving £100. At the same time it must be stated that he received from the Government several grants of land, which in process of time became a source of considerable revenue.

---

[*] S. P. G. Records, p. 142. [†] Do.

The second United-Empire-Loyalist clergyman who came to Canada from the revolted Provinces was the Reverend John Bryan. He is not mentioned by Hawkins,* nor does his name appear in Sabine.† The earliest notice I have seen of him is in a letter from Marsh to General Haldimand, dated the 10th of October, 1780,‡ and written from St. Johns, near Montreal. This letter states that seventy-three Loyalists have arrived, mostly women and children, whose fathers are in the King's service, and that the Rev. Mr. Bryan is with them. The next day the newly-arrived clergyman wrote to Matthews, announcing his escape from the persecution he had long suffered on account of his loyalty. He declares his desire to serve the Loyalists in every way possible, and requests, if agreeable at head-quarters, to be appointed chaplain to Jessup's Corps, which was then being organized.§ The same day, Eben Jessup wrote to Matthews, recommending him for the office in the Corps which he was then raising.‖ On the 16th of October, General Haldimand instructed Monsell to issue provisions to the Rev. Mr. Bryan and his family "the same as to the other Loyalists.** The same day Matthews answered Jessup to the effect that when his Corps should be completed, Mr. Bryan should be appointed to the chaplaincy,†† and Mr. Bryan was assured that "his wishes will be carried out: he will receive the appointment as soon as the corps is completed,' and in the meantime he will be supplied with provisions for his family.‡‡

Although General Haldimand was unwilling to act on the information supplied by Mr. Bryan,§§ yet he treated him with marked consideration and received his warmest thanks in return for his great kindness.‖‖ Among the many letters from Mr. Bryan preserved in the Record Office there is one of the 21st of January, 1781, asking for a ration for a servant,*** and on the 21st of December, nearly a year later, there is one written from Vercheres to the Governor, in

---

* Annals of the Diocese of Quebec.
† Biographical Sketches of Loyalists of the American Revolution, by Lorenzo Sabine.
‡ Can. Arch., Ser. B, Vol. 161, p. 150.
§ Do., Vol. 161, p. 153.
‖ Do. Vol. 161, p. 154.
** Do., Vol. 133, p. 252.
†† Do., Vol. 163, p. 47.
‡‡ Do. Vol. 163, p. 49.
§§ Do., page 48.
‖‖ Do., Vol. 161, page 211.
*** Do., page 232.

which he draws his attention to a promise made him of the appointment to the chaplaincy of Jessup's Corps, and curiously adds that he trusts " His Excellency will not forget poor Joseph, as is asserted the chief butler did after he was restored to his office again."*

Towards the end of 1783, owing to the treaty of peace having been signed, Major Jessup received orders to desist from completing his Corps, and to disband his troops.† Mr. Bryan was then appointed as pastor at New Oswegatchie (Prescott), and a paper on the *State of Religion*, belonging to this period, gives the number of families to whom he ministered at Oswegatchie as forty-four.‡ Some time afterwards Mr. Bryan was appointed to the charge of New Johnstown (Cornwall). There is a letter from Lord Dorchester, the Governor, to Lord Sydney, of the 24th of October, 1787, in which it is stated that temporary grants have been made to New Oswegatchie and Cornwall, but with the intimation that they are only to continue till the settlers can support a clergyman themselves. He also mentions Haldimand's intention of appointing Mr. Bryan to the chaplaincy of Jessup's Corps.§ Accompanying the paper referred to on the *State of Religion*, is a *Clergy List* and *Pay Roll*, in which Mr. Bryan's name figures as Incumbent of Cornwall, and receiving from the Government a stipend of £50 per annum.‖

The next clergyman who came to reside in Canada, also a Loyalist, was the Reverend Dr. John Stuart, whose epitaph in St. George's Cathedral, Kingston, fitly describes as *The Father of the Church of England in Upper Canada*. Hawkins gives 1736 as the year of his birth, and states that he was born in the *Province of Virginia*. Sabine says 1740. With the latter agrees the epitaph already referred to. But a paper in the *Canadian Church Magazine and Mission News* of July, 1891, states that he was born in the year 1730 at Harrisburg, Pennsylvania.

This paper informs us that John Stuart was the son of an Irishman who emigrated to America with the English Colony. He graduated at a Philadelphia College about 1766, and although his parents were strict Presbyterians, he became a member of the Church

---

* Can. Archiv., Series B, Vol. 161, page 357.
† Do., Vol. 163, page 182.
‡ Do., Series Q, Vol. 49, page 343.
§ Can. Arch., Series Q, Vol. 28, page 161.
‖ Do., Vol. 45-2, pages 436-439.

of England. In 1770 he was ordained by Dr. Terrick, Bishop of London. Soon afterwards, Mr. Stuart was appointed to the charge of the Mohawk Mission at Fort Hunter. " On the arrival of the Rev. J. Stuart, 1770, he was enabled, with the assistance of the Sachems, to stop the vice of intemperance in a great degree, and to effect great improvements in their morals. . . When at home the Mohawks regularly attended service daily, and when out hunting, some would come 60 miles to communicate on Christmas Day."* A warm friendship at once sprang up between him and the Chief Tyendinaga, or Joseph Brant, and their friendship bore fruit in the translation of the Gospel of St. Mark and the Book of Common Prayer into the Mohawk language. " Whilst the Mohawks remained at Fort Hunter, the Rev. J. Stuart continued to officiate as usual, performing the public service entire, even after the Declaration of Independence, notwithstanding that by so doing he incurred the penalty of high treason, by the new laws. But as soon as his protectors were fled, he was made a prisoner, and ordered to depart the Province with his family within four days, on peril of being put into close confinement, and with much difficulty he obtained leave to remove to Canada."†

The *Report on Canadian Archives* for 1889 states that " At the breaking out of the American Revolutionary War, he was put under arrest for his loyalty, as is shown by a letter from Schenectady, dated the 29th November, 1780, to Sir John Johnson, in which he says that having been a prisoner on parole for two years, he had at last obtained permission to be exchanged for Mr. Gordon, of Ball's Town, so that he might proceed to the British Provinces." ‡ This exchange, however, was not effected. The Government found his presence at Schenectady too useful to admit of any exchange. Sir John Johnson now looked to Stuart for the information " Hudibras" had formerly supplied, and Haldimand seems to have procured from him regular supplies of " rebel newspapers." § Even as late as the 30th of July, 1781, the governor declared to Sir John Johnson that " The idea of exchanging Mr. Stuart for Colonel Gordon is out of the question. The esteem in which his people hold him will save him from injury, and he may be very useful to us

---

* Pascoe's Digest of S. P. G. Reports, page 73.
† Do., page 74.
‡ Page xxi.
§ Do. xxi.

where he is."* However, his position became unbearable, and eventually he succeeded in effecting an exchange for some American prisoners then held in Canada. By this movement, he forfeited his possessions, and also a sum of four hundred pounds.† The following October he was in Canada.

There is a letter from him to Dr. Smyth from Crown Point, written on the 5th of October, 1781, announcing his arrival with several families, about fifty persons altogether. There were no boats to convey them to Canada.‡ The next day Colonel St. Leger wrote to Matthews, announcing the arrival of a flag at Crown Point, with the Rev. Mr. Stuart, fourteen women, and thirty-nine children.§ Chambers also wrote to General Haldimand on the same subject, also Mr. Blacket, who says that they cannot be received on board the *Carleton*, on account of their baggage. But the *Trumbull* had been dispatched for them.∥

On the 10th of October, Mr. Stuart informed General Haldimand that he had arrived at St. Johns from Schenectady. The news he brings is to the effect that Washington had crossed the Hudson with the French and continentals, and was about to cross the Chesapeake by way of Philadelphia; Cornwallis had landed troops at Point Comfort on York River; Lafayette was near Yorktown; the French fleet had entered the Chesapeake; the British fleet had left Sandy Hook for the Chesapeake; the rebels were expecting a decisive action; and Heath was then with the New England troops at Peekskill.**

In November we find Mr. Stuart in Montreal, where he had opened a public school †† in conjunction with a Mr. Christie. In acknowledging Mr. Stuart's letter containing an advertisement of the school, General Haldimand offered to give every encouragement to so laudable an undertaking, and he appropriated towards its maintenance part of the government grant allowed for such enterprises. There was one expression, however, in the paper to which he dissented. He did not like the words, "Principally intended for the children of Protestants." He took exception to these words, as

---

* Can. Arch., Series B, Vol. 159, p. 153.
† Canadian Church Magazine, July, 1891.
‡ Can. Arch., Series B, Vol. 176, p. 299.
§ Do., Vol. 134, p. 149.
∥ Do., Vol. 142, p. 114.
** Do., Vol. 176, p. 304.
†† Do , Vol. 74, p. 208.

they were likely to cause jealousies. All classes, he held, should be received with equal readiness.* With this injunction Mr. Stuart readily and gladly complied.† In fact he had already admitted to the school Protestants, Roman Catholics and Jews on an equal footing, and he had no desire to make any distinction between pupils on the score of religion.‡

The first English school opened at Montreal was taught by John Pullman, a New Yorker, who had undertaken it at the request of Dr. Ogilvie, who acted on behalf of gentlemen residing in Montreal.§ This school, opened in 1773, was maintained until 1782, when Mr. Pullman was obliged to seek employment as a clerk,‖ which he found at the St. Maurice Forges. Here he remained for the rest of his life, dying on the 13th of August, 1804.** Finlay Fisher and a Mr. Christie had also opened schools at Montreal, before the arrival of John Stuart,†† but they appear to have been unsatisfactory. Mr. Stuart's school was the first successful attempt at supplying the English youth of Montreal with a liberal education. His school, however, was opened in conjunction with Mr. Christie, who was employed to teach Mathematics and the ordinary English branches. They had scarcely begun operations when Mr. Christie's thorough incompetency became painfully apparent. In his School Report, dated the 27th of November, 1782, Mr. Stuart stated that his assistant was unable to teach even the lowest branches. He knew nothing of the Classics, and even of his own subjects, of which he professed to be a perfect master, he knew absolutely nothing. " I could have dispensed with his ignorance of the English language even, and his faulty accent," he writes to General Haldimand, " but when I found him unacquainted with the rules of common Arithmetic, and often obliged to apply to me in the presence of the pupils for the solution of the most simple questions, I could no longer doubt of his inefficiency." ‡‡ Mr. Christie was accordingly dismissed, and a new assistant engaged. At that period his school

---

* Can. Arch., Series B., Vol. 159, p. 165.
† Do. Vol. 158, p. 257.
‡ Do.
§ Report on Canadian Archives, 1889, p. 20.
‖ Do.
** Parish Register, Three Rivers.
†† Report Can. Arch. 1889, p. 20.
‡‡ Canadian Archives, Series B, Vol. 152, p. 281.

numbered forty-four pupils, and there was every prospect of an increased attendance.

Mr. Stuart, during his residence at Montreal, acted as deputy chaplain of the 60th Regiment. We have already noticed his letter to General Haldimand, stating that Mr. Doty's half-pay was an important addition to his small income. He also assisted Mr. Delisle, to the edification of the English residents. A paper on the *State of Religion in Canada* * of the period contains the following: " The greater part of the Inhabitants at Montreal are Presbyterians of the Church of Scotland. These being weary of attending a Minister whom they did not understand, and for other reasons, have established a Presbyterian Minister, and subscribed liberally to his support. His name is Bethune,† and he was late Chaplain to the 84th Regiment, and while Mr. Stuart assisted Mr. Delisle (which he did for a short time) he used constantly to attend the Services of our Church."

But Mr. Stuart had no desire to remain at Montreal. In February, 1784, he requested the appointment of chaplain to the garrison at Cataraqui.‡ Receiving a favourable reply, he engaged a substitute for his school-work, and made arrangements for devoting the early part of the summer to a visit through the principal part of his new mission. Few men would contemplate the great field without dismay, with all our modern facilities for travelling; and we can thoroughly admire the earnestness of such a man who in such a cause could ignore the peculiar difficulties of the time and place.

He travelled as far westward as Niagara, leaving Montreal on the 2nd of June, "visiting on his way all the new settlements of Loyalists on the river and lake, and on the 18th arrived at Niagara. On the following Sunday he preached in the garrison, and in the afternoon, to satisfy the eager expectations of the Mohawks, he proceeded on horseback to their village, about nine miles distant, and officiated in their church. After a short intermission, they returned to their church, where he baptised 78 infants and 5 adults. The whole was concluded with a discourse on the nature and design of baptism." § " I never felt more pleasing sensations," he wrote to the S. P. G. in his report of this visit, "than on this solemn occa-

---
* Can. Arch., Series Q, Vol. 49, p. 343.
† The late Bishop of Toronto and the late Dean of Montreal were sons of this gentleman.
‡ Can. Arch. Series B, Vol. 165, p. 175.
§ Pascoe's Digest of S. P. G. Reports, page 154.

sion. To see those affectionate people from whom I had been separated more than seven years, assembled in a decent commodious church, erected principally by themselves, behaving themselves with the greatest outward devotion and becoming gravity, filled my heart with joy." We can imagine the satisfaction with which he ministered to his old parishioners, and dispensed once more the Bread of Life, using the venerable altar service he had last seen in the little stone church at Fort Hunter.*

This was the most extensive missionary journey yet undertaken by any Anglican clergyman in Canada. From the Mohawk village near Niagara, he visited every encampment of Loyalists and friendly Indians as far eastward as Coteau du Lac, ministering to all alike, and baptizing as many as one hundred and fifty people.† We can now form but a very imperfect idea of the peculiar difficulties which such a journey entailed, as all the country over which he journeyed was for the most part an unexplored region.

As soon as it was definitely arranged that Mr. Stuart should settle at Kingston (Cataraqui), he gave up his school at Montreal, and entered heartily into the duties of his new sphere of usefulness. On the 30th of October, 1784, Major Matthews informed him that the Government desired him to influence Captain John, an Indian Chief then at Cataraqui, to join the rest of the Six Nations at the Grand River, and to take his people with him. He could promise to visit them every now and then, and watch over the progress in education and morals of their Indian youths.‡ Thus in 1785 Mr. Stuart, accompanied by his wife—who was a daughter of Governor Dinwiddie of Virginia, and his three sons, arrived at Kingston, the scene of his future labours. He was granted 200 acres of land lying at the west side of the town, and later some more valuable limits.§ His new mission was a very extensive one, embracing several townships, which he visited periodically,‖ and yet he was able, the following year,** to establish and maintain for many years with eminent success the first English school attempted in Upper Canada.††

---

* The late Bishop Mountain, in a report to the Earl of Durham, dated the 20th Nov., 1838, says, "The Mohawks preserve to this day, with much veneration, a set of Communion Plate and other appendages of divine worship, which were given them by Queen Anne when they were seated in the Colonies which now form part of the United States of America."
† Can. Arch., Series B, Vol. 162, page 333.
‡ Do., Vol. 64, page 370.
§ Can. Miss. Mag., July, 1891, p. 156.
‖ Langtry's Eastern Canada and New Foundland, p. 231.
** McCord's Canadian Dates.
†† An Indian school had already been established by Sir John Johnson at the Mohawk Village

We have a few notices of the Reverend George Gilmore, although his name does not appear in any work on the Loyalists I have seen, and he was not in charge of any mission in Canada.

The references I have collected concerning him are as follows:

January 25, 1783.—Dr. George Smith wrote to headquarters from St. Johns, near Montreal, stating that he had received a petition from George Gilmore, who reports the endurance of much distress owing to his loyalty.*

March 13.—General Riedesel wrote to General Haldimand from Sorel, informing him that Mr. Gilmore had been received as schoolmaster at St. Johns, and that the English-speaking inhabitants had raised a subscription for him of £48 a year.†

March 22,—Dr. Smyth wrote to General Riedesel, from St. Johns, that he would use his influence to make Mr. Gilmore's situation as confortable as possible.‡

May 20.—Mr. Gilmore wrote to Captain Matthews, stating that he had sent his memorial already. He claims that he is entitled to assistance, and he hopes that the petition of the people of St. Johns in his favour as prospective school-master will be granted.§

May 31.—Mr. Gilmore memorialized the Government from Quebec, praying that an allowance may be granted to him to enable him to perform clerical duties in the Bay of Chaleurs.||

Finally, the *Quebec Gazette* of the 15th of January, 1784, contains this item:—

SOREL, Dec. 29, 1783.

Saturday last being the anniversary of St. John the Evangelist, the Lodge at this place met at the Lodge Room, and from thence proceeded to the School Room, where an excellent sermon suitable to the day was preached by the Reverend Mr. Gilmore, after which they returned to the lodge-room again, where an elegant entertainment was provided, and the following truly loyal and Masonic Toasts were drank..........

The name of the Reverend Samuel Peters, a Loyalist from Connecticut, will come before us in connection with the Episcopal appointment to the See of Quebec. He does not appear to have performed any clerical duty in Canada.

---

* Can. Arch., Series B, Vol. 134, page 251.
† Do., Vol. 138, p. 168.
‡ Do., p. 185.
§ Do., Vol. 162, p. 44.
|| Do., Vol. 162, page 44.

CHAPTER VI.

THE THREE ENGLISH CLERGYMEN.

REFERENCE has already been made to the Reverend Mr. Toosey. By his *Letter of Orders*, preserved in the Archives of the Cathedral at Quebec, we learn that the Reverend Philip Toosey was educated at Trinity Hall, Cambridge, and that he was ordained by " Philip, Bishop of Norwich," in Park Street Chapel, near Grosvenor Square, Westminster, on Sunday, the 19th of February, 1769.

In 1784, whilst at Stonham, he made arrangements to take up the work in Canada to which the Rev. Mr. Guerry had been appointed ten years before.* On May 27th, Mr. Toosey informed Governor Haldimand, by letter, that he could not sail for Quebec till the following spring. He wants some land, he says, and is anxious that his sons should enter the service as volunteers. He intends to take out with him some improved cattle, agricultural implements, etc., and would also take with him labourers, skilled workmen, and mechanics if he could get land for them.†

At the end of July, 1785, Mr. Toosey and his family arrived at Quebec, from London, on the ship "Charlotte," after a voyage of fifty-five days.‡ A paper on the *State of Religion*, drawn up, it appears, in 1786, after mentioning Mr. Guerry's return to England, says that "Last year, the Reverend Mr. Toosey, who has two livings in Suffolk, was sent in his room, without being appointed to any settled place wherein to officiate as a clergyman,"§ and it suggests : " As Mr. Toosey has no fixed employment, and is an Englishman, might not he be directed to officiate either at Quebec, or Montreal, or Trois Rivières, where it is presumed that churches ought to be built ? "

As Mr. Doty had been appointed to Sorel, and there were no vacancies in any of the parishes, and no new ones ready to be established, it was arranged that Mr. Toosey should take up some English work at Quebec. We have no means of knowing whether

---

* Can. Arch., Series B, Vol. 75-2, page 82.
† Do., page 114.
‡ *Quebec Gazette*, 28th July, 1785.
§ Can. Arch., Series Q, Vol. 49, page 343.

Mr. De Montmollin still declined to receive assistance from English clergymen; but we do not find Mr. Toosey's name in the Quebec Parish Register until 1789. Two years before this date, however, he had shown sufficient zeal in the discharge of his duties in the vicinity of Quebec to meet the warm commendation of Lord Dorchester (Sir Guy Carleton), Governor, who thus speaks of him in a letter to Lord Sydney, Colonial Secretary: " The exemplary manners, discretion and abilities of Mr. Toosey cannot be passed in silence; he is recommended to notice." *

Similar commendations continued to flow into the Colonial Office for some years. As Mr. Toosey's name will come very prominently before us in connection with the Bishop of Nova Scotia's visitation, and the appointment of the first Bishop of Quebec, it will be unnecessary to dwell more fully here upon him and his interesting work.

The Reverend James Marmaduke Tunstall was one of the foremost figures of his day in the Church in Lower Canada.

He was born at Kendal, Westmoreland, England, in the year 1760. He was educated at Oxford, and, after his ordination, came to Canada in 1787, under the auspices of the *Society for the Propagation of the Gospel*, and by the appointment of Lord Dorchester.

On his arrival in Canada, Mr. Tunstall was appointed to the new mission of St. Armand, where a large number of Protestants had already found a home. There is a letter in the Record Office from Dr. Morice, Secretary of the S. P. G., bearing the date 26th November, 1788, to Nepean,† informing him that two clergymen, Mr. John Langhorne and Mr. John (James) Tunstall had been sent to the Province of Quebec as missionaries, relying on Lord Dorchester to pay them the same allowance as that made to Mr. Stuart and Mr. Doty. His Lordship has had no instructions to do so. The hardships endured by the missionaries on this account are then alluded to, and it is requested that instructions be sent to pay the usual allowances. This was complied with, as we learn from a letter from Lord Grenville to Lord Dorchester, dated Whitehall, February 20, 1790, authorizing him to pay Messrs. Langhorne and Tunstall the same stipend as Stuart and Doty, and also the arrears of pay since their arrival in the Province.‡

---

* Can. Arch., Series Q, Vol. 28, page 161.
† Can. Arch., Series Q, Vol. 38, page 386.
‡ Do., Vol. 44-1, page 1.

The Reverend John Langhorne was born in Wales, educated at St. Bees College,* ordained in England, and appointed Curate of Hartwell in the Diocese of Chester.†

Under the auspices of the S. P. G., Mr. Langhorne came to Canada in 1787, probably in company with Mr. Tunstall.‡ He experienced many difficulties in reaching his destination. He was detained at Quebec, and was at last glad to make arrangements for his journey to Kingston on board a sloop charged with a cargo of government stores. As there were upwards of one hundred barrels of gunpowder on board, no fires were allowed to be lighted, and the sloop grounded in shallow water long before reaching Montreal. Twelve days had been spent between Quebec and Montreal, and Mr. Langhorne decided to accomplish the rest of his journey by any means that presented themselves, anything being preferable to the sloop. As there were no public conveyances, he walked to Lachine, and thence up the St. Lawrence, either walking or slowly propelled in an open boat. One night he slept in a hay loft, another on a deal floor, without even a blanket to cover him. "Another night," he says, "I had my abode in the woods; but I could not lie down as it rained." Thus he proceeded all the way, arriving at last at Kingston, where Mr. Stuart was already stationed.§

Mr. Langhorne was at once appointed to the charge of the country about the Bay of Quinté, with his headquarters at Ernestown. The first year of his incumbency, he had 1,500 souls in his charge, baptized 107 children and adults, and within five years, succeeded in opening eight places of worship in his parish. These were St. Oswald's, St. Cuthbert's, St. Warburg's, St. Thomas's, St. Paul's, St. John's, St. Peter's and St. Luke's. ||

As in all other cases in Canada, except the first three parishes, there was much difficulty, and long and tedious delays in procuring the grants promised by the Government. Thus, Lord Dorchester writes to Lord Sydney, on the 24th of October, 1787, that "Mr. Langhorne has £50 from the S. P. G.;"** but making no mention of

---

* Eastern Can. and Newfoundland, p. 232.
† S. P. G. Records, p. 875.
‡ Can. Arch., Series Q, Vol. 38, page 386.
§ Eastern Canada and Newfoundland, pp. 232-3.
|| S. P. G. Records, p. 155.
** Can. Arch., Series Q, Vol. 28, page 161.

any prospective grant from the Government. Then Dr. Morice writes to Nepean, on the 26th of November, 1788, as we have seen, urging the payment of the usual allowances. Nothing being done for his relief, he again writes on the 20th of July, 1789, calling attention to the case of the "Reverend John Langhorne starving at Ernestown on £50 a year." * And yet no authorization was sent to the Governor to pay the promised grants until the 20th of February, 1790.

---

*Can. Arch., Series Q, Vol. 43-1, page 776.

CHAPTER VII.

THE BISHOP OF NOVA SCOTIA'S VISITATION.

THE visitation of the Bishop of Nova Scotia must be regarded as one of the turning points of the history of the Church of England in Canada.

"Dr. Inglis had been first a Missionary of the Propagation Society at Dover, in Delaware, and later became an Assistant Minister, and still later, in March, 1783, the Rector of Trinity Church, New York. He was the intimate friend of Seabury, the first Bishop consecrated for this Continent.........A Republican historian of New York, writing of those troublous times, tells us, how Dr. Inglis 'was forbidden by its citizens to pray for the King and the Royal family,' and how, 'finally,' his life was threatened if he did not desist from using the Liturgy according to the text. 'To officiate publicly,' continues the same writer, 'and yet abstain from the mention of England's monarch in his supplications, was to violate his oath, and the dictates of his own conscience. His embarrassment was very great. One Sunday morning, a company of one hundred and fifty men marched into the church with drums beating and pipes playing, and bayonets glistening in their loaded guns. The congregation was terror-stricken, and women fainted. It was supposed that if Dr. Inglis should read the Collects for the King and Royal family he would be shot in the sacred desk. But he went on boldly to the end, omitting no portion of the service, and, like Daniel, prayed as he did aforetime.' (Lamb's History of the City of New York, Vol. II, Part I., page 85). That was good stuff to make a Bishop of, and in due time his Sovereign found it out! The Vestry closed Trinity Church, New York, soon after this incident, and, in the year 1783, Dr. Inglis resigned his Rectorship and removed from New York to Halifax, and four years later was consecrated Bishop."*

The Patent conferring ecclesiastical jurisdiction over the Provinces of Quebec, New Brunswick and Newfoundland, upon Dr. Inglis, reads as follows :—

---

* Bishop Potter's Sermon at the Centenary of the Diocese of Quebec, June 1, 1893.

GEORGE THE THIRD, to Charles Inglis, Bishop of Nova Scotia:

WHEREAS, our Provinces of Quebec, New Brunswick and Newfoundland are not yet divided, or formed into Dioceses as Bishop's Sees, by reason whereof the jurisdiction in causes ecclesiastical arising within the said Provinces is solely vested in us as Supreme Head on earth of the Church of England within our Dominions, and it seems necessary to us that the Episcopal functions should be performed, and the spiritual and ecclesiastical jurisdiction should from henceforth be administered and executed in the said Provinces in the cases in these presents hereafter mentioned by our Royal Authority, according to the laws and Canons of the Church of England, which are lawfully held and received in England.

KNOW that we, having great confidence in your learning, morals, probity and prudence, have given and granted, and by these presents do give and grant unto you, the aforesaid Bishop of Nova Scotia, full power and authority, by yourself, and by your sufficient commissary or commissaries to be by you instituted and appointed, to exercise jurisdiction spiritual and ecclesiastical in the aforesaid Provinces, or respectively, according to the laws and Canons of the Church of England, which are lawfully made and received in England in the several causes and matters hereafter in these presents expressed and specified, and no other, and for a declaration of our royal will concerning the special causes and matters in which we will that the aforesaid episcopal functions shall be performed, and the aforesaid spiritual and ecclesiastical jurisdiction shall be exercised by virtue of this Commission, we have further given and granted to you, the Bishop of Nova Scotia, full power and authority to confer the Orders of Deacon and Priest upon persons of the said Provinces, &c., &c.*

We are assured in *Eastern Canada and Newfoundland*, that "There is no record of any visit ever having been paid by Bishop Inglis to Canada."† This assertion, published in a popular work on the Canadian Church, coupled with the importance necessarily attached to the first Episcopal visitation of any Colony, appears to call for fuller details of Dr. Inglis' visit to Canada than would otherwise be required.

---

* I am indebted to the Very Rev. Edwin Gilpin, D.D., Dean of Nova Scotia, for a copy of this document.
† Page 28.

The Memoir of the late Bishop Mountain, written by his son, the late Armine W. Mountain, is a very trustworthy book, and one well known in Canada. This work thus introduces this visitation :*

"In the whole extent of the Colonial Empire of Great Britain, throughout the world, there was no Bishop of the Church of England before the erection of the Diocese of Nova Scotia, to which the Rev. Dr. Charles Inglis was appointed in 1787. That prelate, acting under powers conferred upon him in his patent from the Crown, visited Canada, and held confirmations as well as a visitation of the clergy, some, if not all of whom, received licenses at his hands in 1789. The whole number of clergymen who could then be assembled from one end of the Province to the other (Upper and Lower Canada having then constituted together the Province of Quebec) was eight. It appears that in 1774, they had been four in number, including a chaplain to the garrison at Quebec."

The Bishop's arrival at Quebec is fully recorded in the *Gazette* :—

"11th June, 1789.

"Tuesday afternoon arrived from Halifax, last from the Island of St. John, his Majesty's Frigate *Dido*, Charles Sandys, Esqre, Commander. In her came the Right Reverend Father-in-God CHARLES, Bishop of Nova Scotia. Yesterday forenoon the Bishop left the *Dido*, accompanied by Captain Sandys, under a salute of eleven guns, and was received on shore by Colonel Davies, Commander of the Garrison, and several other officers, the Reverend Mr. De Montmollin, Rector, and the Reverend Mr. Toosey, minister, of the Church in this city, and several respectable citizens."

Having remained a fortnight at Quebec, during which period the details of his visitation were arranged, Dr. Inglis set out on his trip to Montreal and the intervening parishes. His departure from Quebec is thus briefly alluded to in the *Gazette:*—

"25th June, 1789.

"Yesterday afternoon, at two o'clock, the Right Reverend Bishop of Nova Scotia set out from this city on his way for Montreal."

On the 26th, the Episcopal party reached Three Rivers. The following Sunday, the Bishop preached a sermon in the Recollet

---

* Page 383.

Church, and received a child into the Church. This is the first record I have seen of divine service performed by him, although he probably officiated at Quebec the Sunday before. The baptismal entry is as follows :—

" Le treize de Juin est né John, et a été baptisé le vingt et un du dit mois, fils de John Macpherson et de Marie Cameron, les père et mère. Le vingt et neuf de Juin ont eté supplieur les ceremonies du Baptême par Monseigneur l'eveque de Nouvelle Scotia, à John, fils de John Macpherson et de Marie Cameron, les pere et mere. Le pareins ont le Reverend Mr. Veyssière, Recteur de la paroise, et Colonel John Morris, et la mareine, Anne Charlotte Cameron."

The description of the Bishop's interesting visit to Three Rivers is fully given in the *Quebec Gazette* of the 2nd of July, 1789:—

"THREE RIVERS, June 30.

" Friday afternoon arrived here the Right Reverend Charles Inglis, Bishop of Nova Scotia, who was received by the principal British inhabitants with the greatest demonstrations of joy, and on Sunday he preached an excellent sermon. The Form of Prayer and Thanksgiving prepared by His Grace the Archbishop of Canterbury was used upon this joyful occasion, which was attended by the principal inhabitants, both French and English, of this town, and in the evening was sung the *Te Deum* by His Majesty's Roman Catholic subjects in the Parish Church, as a thanksgiving to Almighty God for the recovery of His Majesty's health. The same having been announced at divine service in the forenoon by the Reverend Mr. St. Onge, Grand Vicaire, was attended by all the principal inhabitant of the place. And on Monday morning, was given by the Right Reverend CHARLES INGLIS, Bishop of Nova Scotia, to the Reverend Messrs. Vessier (Veyssière) and St. Onge, to be distributed to the poor, one hundred loaves of Bread. And about nine o'clock he set out on his journey for Montreal."

The Bishop's visit to Montreal is thus related in the *Gazette* of the 16th of July :—

" MONTREAL, July 9.

" On Thursday evening last (3d inst.) arrived here from Quebec, the Right Reverend Father-in-God, CHARLES, Bishop of Nova Scotia. The Bishop was met at Pointe aux Trembles, and conducted into the city, and has since received the compliments of the most respectable inhabitants both of the Protestant and Romish persuasions. On Sunday morning he delivered to a numerous auditory an excellent discourse on the nature and end of Confirmation, with a view to the administration of that ordinance next Sunday. And yesterday he received and answered the following Address from the Rector, Church Wardens, and Protestant inhabitants of this city :—

"'To the Right Reverend Father in God, CHARLES, NOVA SCOTIA, &c., &c. :

" The Rector, Church Wardens, and Protestant inhabitants of the city of Montreal, beg leave to congratulate you on your safe arrival in Canada, where their wishes invited you, and where your presence fills every heart well affected to the Church and State with joy and comfort.

" Sensible, Right Reverend Sir, of the vast benefits that must accrue to this country by the encouragement of true religion, piety, virtue, and learning, we are happy in the prospect of seeing them flourish under your spiritual care and patronage : in that light, we view your appointment as one of those distinguished blessings which Divine Providence confers on a favoured people ; and we acknowledge with the highest gratitude His Majesty's perpetual care and bounty, in placing at the head of the flock a pastor and governor so eminent for his merit and abilities. The smiling prospect before us gives us the joyful hope of seeing the Protestant Church in Canada emerging from obscurity, and acquiring under your auspices the full enjoyment of her rights ; and that the seeds of knowledge and truth, cultivated and cherished by your propitious hands, will disseminate and produce the fairest fruits.

" We beg leave, Right Reverend Sir, to assure you of our earnest desire to concur with zeal and alacrity in support of our Holy Faith, well convinced that her principles tend to the Glory of God, and to the welfare and happiness of mankind.

" We have the honour, with most profound respect,
RIGHT REVEREND SIR,
Your most obedient and humble servants,
DAVID CH'D. DELISLE, Rector.
JAMES HALLOWELL,
ADAM SCOTT,   } Church Wardens.
JAMES NOEL,

John Johnson, Joseph Frobisher, Edward Wm. Gray, James McGill, Dumas St. Martin, James Finlay, John A. Gray, Thomas Forsyth, J. Walker, John Gray, William Jones, Henry Leodel, Joseph Howard, J. M. Mayer, T. Walker, James Dunlop, John Lilly, Wm. Hunter, John Platt, Chas. Bordevine, Wm. Nelson, Robert Mell, Finlay Fisher, John Turner, J. Turner, jr., Jer. Geo. Turner, G. Young, Jacob Kuhn, Wm. Clarke, James Perry, Robert Sym, James Cuthbertson, John Bell, Peter Arnoldi, John McArthur, Robert Simpson, Thomas Oakes, James Deyer White, Geo. Stansfield, J. Fraser, John Burke, Alex'r Henry, J. G. Beek, Isaac W. Clarke, Edw'd Southouse, Thos. Busby, Conrad Morsteller, Thos. Rudenhurst, James Hughes, R. Cruickshanks, John Devereux, Thomas McMurray, John Russel, Chas. Blake, Josiah Pomeroy, W. England, Christopher Fournier, Michael Cook, John Daly, Benjamin Holmes, John Mittleberger, Samuel David, W. H. McNeil, R. Jones, James Morrison, John McGill, James Laing, Henry Gonnerman, Fred Gonnerman, J. Schiefflin, John Kay, Wm. Kay, Dan'l Robertson. Montreal, June 17, 1789."

To this address the Bishop made the following reply :—

GENTLEMEN,

Permit me to return my sincere thanks for your very kind congratulations ; and to assure you that I have the liveliest sense of this, and of the other marks of polite attention with which the Rector, Church Wardens, and Protestant inhabitants of the city of Montreal have been pleased to honour me.

Anxious as I truly am that His Majesty's beneficent views may be answered in appointing a Protestant Bishop for his American dominions, it gives me unspeakable pleasure to find that you entertain such just sentiments of the advantages which accrue to society by encouraging true Religion and learning ; and to be assured of your " earnest desire to concur, with zeal and alacrity, in support of our Holy Faith, from a conviction of its tendency to promote the glory of God, and the happiness of mankind."

These sentiments, and this disposition, do you the highest honour. They manifest a laudable concern for the welfare of posterity, the interest and reputation of your country, the credit of our most Holy Religion, and the honour of Him Who is the great Author of our existence, and of all other mercies. You may believe me when I assure you, that no endeavour on my part shall be wanting to promote objects so important; and that I shall reckon it among the happiest circumstances of my life, if my endeavours, in connection with yours, should be crowned with success. Attention to Religion and Literature will ever mark the conduct of a wise people. Religion is the only sure basis of virtue; as virtue is the source of public prosperity. The inward purity, benevolence, and rectitude of morals so strongly inculcated by Christianity, at once secure the happiness of individuals, and are productive of general order and peace in communities. And from science are derived all those improvements which contribute so much to the convenience of life; and that superiority by which enlightened nations are distinguished from those that are sunk in ignorance and barbarism.

I see no just cause to doubt, but much reason to believe, that, with the blessing of God on such prudent measures as shall be adopted for the purpose, our joint efforts may assure those benefits to this Province. Under the patronage of our beloved Sovereign, and of his worthy representative in British America, there is every incentive to animate your exertions. And whilst you manifest a becoming zeal for the truths and duties of our Holy Faith, and for the advancement of Literature, I trust that zeal will always be tempered with such mildness and candour towards others, as shall evince you to be genuine followers of Him Who has declared that Mutual Love is the distinguishing badge and characteristic of His Disciples.

I cannot forbear, on this occasion, most heartily to congratulate you on the late memorable event, which may serve to stimulate your zeal in the business before us—I mean His Majesty's recovery from a dangerous and afflicting illness. No people, perhaps, were ever more blessed than we in a Sovereign, who is anxiously solicitous for the happiness of his subjects, who is the munificent Patron of science, and who exhibits in his own person a shining example of every Christian and princely virtue. But we were lately alarmed with dismal apprehensions that this blessing would be snatched from us— the whole nation was overspread with gloom—distress appeared in every countenance—sympathetic sorrow pervaded every bosom— all were deeply interested in the preservation of their common benefactor and Father, and offered their fervent petition to Heaven for his recovery. God has been graciously pleased to hear us, and to restore our much beloved Sovereign to the prayers of his people.

It remains for us that we cherish a grateful sense of so transcendent a mercy, and testify the sincerity of our gratitude by acts of devout homage to the Almighty, and by unshaken loyalty to our Sovereign. May His subjects long, very long and thankfully enjoy the blessings of His mild and just government; and may the citizens of Montreal, in particular, prosperous and crowned with all temporal felicity, exhibit such a pattern of warm attention to the interests of religion, virtue and science, as shall excite emulation and similar exertions in their fellow-subjects throughout the Province of Quebec.

Heartily commending you to the grace and protection of Almighty God, I am, with sentiments of sincere esteem,

GENTLEMEN, your affectionate and humble servant,

CHARLES NOVA SCOTIA.

Montreal, July 8, 1789.

For some years the services of the Church at Montreal had been held at the Recollet Church, and the congregation were very desirous of having a church of their own. They accordingly referred this subject to Dr. Inglis, at the same time praying him to appoint an English assistant to Mr. Delisle, offering to raise £100 by subscription toward his support. The result of this application was the permission to use the chapel of the Jesuits, which was granted by the Government, and the appointment of Mr. Tunstall as assistant minister. These transactions are of sufficient consequence to justify the reproduction from the pages of *The Canadian Magazine* of 1825 (Vol. IV., pp. 218-224) of part of the article entitled "An Account of Christ's Church in the City of Montreal," which refers to these important changes, and contains the Bishop's reply to the application of the Rector and Wardens.*

"As yet there was no church or place in which divine worship could be performed, and the limited numbers of the congregation and their circumscribed means precluded the possibility of their building a suitable church for the present. This obstacle was happily got over by an application to the Recollets for the use of their church for Mr. Delisle to officiate in, at such hours as they might not themselves have occasion for it; and it deserves to be

---

* I am indebted to my friend F. C. Wurtele, Esq., Secretary of the Quebec Literary and Historical Society, for a copy of this article.

mentioned as a proof of the liberal feelings of that body that they readily complied with that application. This deficit being supplied for the time, the service of the Church of England was regularly performed by Mr. Delisle. In the month of July, 1789, the Rt. Rev. Charles, Bishop of Nova Scotia, came to Canada on a Diocesan visitation ; and the Protestant Episcopal congregation in Montreal, now considerably augmented in numbers, availed themselves of this event, and made several applications to him for some requisites they stood in need of, in order to place themselves on a more respectable and permanent footing. Mr. Delisle, being now considerably advanced in years, and less able to discharge the increasing duties of his station, they applied to the Bishop, praying that an assistant might be appointed to him : at the same time, the congregation bound themselves to raise by subscription the sum of £100 per annum to pay the salary of that assistant. In the same address, bearing date the 15th day of July, 1789, the congregation represented the inconvenience they suffered from the want of a place of worship for themselves : and prayed the Bishop to use his influence with Lord Dorchester, then Governor-in-Chief of the Province, whom they had also petitioned for a church which formerly belonged to the Jesuits' College, and stood near where the present gaol is built ; but which had, at the time we mention, become the property of Government by the extinction of the Order of Jesuits in Montreal. They, in addition to these requests, petitioned the Government for assistance to enable them to put this church in a state of repair. The petition expressive of these desires was presented to his Reverence the Bishop, by Messrs. Hallowell, Noel and Scott, as Church-Wardens, and was crowned with the wished-for success, as will be seen from the following letter from the Bishop in reply to it, which was read to the congregation on the 23rd of August, 1789. It is proper to observe that along with the petition to the Governor, there was sent an estimate of the expenses which would be required for finishing the shell of the church, and which was liberally defrayed by Government, leaving the congregation to bear only the burden of fitting up and finishing the inside of it.

QUEBEC, August 10th.

GENTLEMEN :—

I received your letter of the 15th of July, by the Rev. Mr. Delisle, and have the pleasure to inform you that the application for the

Jesuits' church at Montreal has succeeded. Lord Dorchester has approved the last report of expense for repairing the shell, amounting to more than £300, and has given orders to have the repairs done immediately; when finished, the key will be given as I direct. I sincerely congratulate you on this event, and must now request you to set about the necessary measures without loss of time for having the pews, pulpit and reading-desk built, with a small, neat chancel and communion table. You will please to have a proper pew reserved for the Governor. It wi'l be advisable to name one for the Bishop, which he will very seldom use, and may be occupied by some family except when the Bishop is on a visit to Montreal. I beg leave to propose that the church be called CHRIST'S CHURCH. The next thing to be done after procuring the church is to adjust matters between Mr. Delisle and Mr. Tunstall, which I flatter myself is now done so as to preclude future disputes. Mr. Tunstall is a modest, sensible, young man, of good learning and unblemished moral character. His voice is harmonious and strong enough when he exerts it; it will grow stronger by time and exercise. Mr. Delisle remains as he was, the first minister. He is to preach in French at such times as shall be judged expedient. He is also to preach occasionally in English, though not often. Mr. Tunstall is assistant and regular English preacher. He accounts to Mr. Delisle for the stated fees for Marriages and Burials, and no other fees are due; and Mr. Delisle in return is to pay the sum of £20 a year to Mr. Tunstall. Both parties have agreed to these regulations, and I trust they will remove any ground of contest. Let me beseech you and the congregation to preserve order and promote peace; these are characteristics of true Christianity, and are essential to the character of true members of the Church of England. Be it your endeavour to soften and quiet any uneasiness, should any arise; though I have such an opinion of the prudence and good temper of both the gentlemen that I flatter myself there will be no just cause of any on their part. I feel myself peculiarly interested in the prosperity of your congregation. At my late visitation here I thought it advisable to give some INJUNCTIONS to the Clergy; they are printed, and I enclose a copy for your perusal. Some things are recommended to the Church Wardens and vestries of Parishes; and I beg leave to express my wishes that you would follow these recommendations. I think you must see the propriety of them. Mr. Tunstall will repair to Montreal, whenever you judge it necessary. Perhaps it will be time enough when the church is ready for use, which I trust will be the case before winter. He will go up sooner if you desire it, and I sincerely think he will be a great acquisition to you. I heartily recommend you and the congregation to the blessing and protection of Almighty God, and am in great haste,

GENTLEMEN, your affectionate brother, and humble servant,

CHARLES NOVA SCOTIA.

To Messrs.
Hallowell,   } Church Wardens."
Noel & Scott.

I have seen no further record of Dr. Inglis' work at Montreal. On his return to Quebec he seems to have visited Sorel. Canon Anderson, Rector of Sorel, thus refers to this visit in his centenary sermon already alluded to:

"In 1789 Bishop Inglis, of Nova Scotia, the first Protestant Bishop in British North America, visited Quebec and Montreal, and as the old inhabitants of that time all asserted, he stopped a day in passing at Sorel, preaching in the church, and consecrating the Burial-ground. Mr. Jackson was cognizant of this fact, but as it was simply a tradition of what had taken place some fifty years before, with no written record of it whatever in the church books, good old Bishop Stewart, to make assurance doubly sure, consecrated the ground over again in 1834."

As we do not appear to have any record of the Bishop's movements between the 12th of July, when he confirmed at Montreal, and the 5th of August, on which day the Episcopal visitation began at Quebec, there is every probability that he visited Sorel in the meantime, according to the local tradition.

The approaching visitation was the most important conference of the clergy which had yet taken place in Canada. Indeed it may be reckoned as the first, as there does not seem to have been any united action hitherto on the part of the Anglican clergy, except perhaps in an address presented to Sir Guy Carleton on his appointment as governor some twenty years before.* Referring to this visitation, Bishop Mountain wrote as follows: "The whole number of clergymen who could then be assembled from one end of the Province to the other (Upper and Lower Canada having then con-

* *Quebec Gazette*, Nov. 17, 1763.

stituted together the Province of Quebec) was eight."* This number did not include the army chaplains, nor Messrs Scott, Gilmore, and Bryan. There were many serious difficulties encountered by the clergy in attending this conference. Thus Mr. Veyssière had buried his wife on the 24th of July; and Mr. Stuart in company with Mr. Langhorne, to attend this visitation, were obliged to encounter in their trip about eight hundred miles of difficult travelling, an undertaking which required five weeks for its accomplishment.

The record of this famous conference is contained in the *Quebec Gazette* of the issue of the 13th of August, and is as follows:

"On Wednesday, the 5th instant, the Right Reverend Father-in-God CHARLES, Bishop of Nova Scotia, held his primary visitation at the Church of the Recollets in this city. Divine service was performed to a crowded audience, and a sermon was preached by the Revd. Philip Toosey, minister of the parish; after divine service an excellent charge was delivered by the Bishop to his clergy, upon the various and important duties of their office, with great force and energy. On Thursday, divine service was performed and a sermon preached by the Revd. Mr. Stuart, minister of Kingston.

"And on Friday, divine service was performed and a sermon preached by the Revd. Mr. Doty, minister of William Henry; after which the Bishop held a Confirmation, at which upwards of one hundred and thirty were confirmed.

"On Saturday, divine service was again performed and a sermon preached by the Revd. Mr. Tunstall.

"On the Sunday following, the Sacrament was administered by the Bishop himself to a great number of communicants, several of whom had|been previously confirmed ; and in the afternoon, some persons expressing a desire of participating in this ancient and salutary rite of the Christian Church, the Bishop indulged them with a private confirmation."

Bishop Mountain, in the extract from his address to the Second Session of the Quebec Synod, already referred to, asserted that Dr. Inglis issued licences to some if not to all the clergy assembled at his visitation. As far as possible, Dr. Inglis soothed the jarring elements which had so long retarded the progress of the Church. The Bishop's commissary reported to Lord Dorchester that the

---
*Memoir of Bishop Mountain, p. 383.

Swiss clergy were "found incompetent by the Bishop of Nova Scotia to read and preach in English," and that they "do no duty, there being no Canadian Protestants to form a congregation." Mr. Veyssière, however, "for want of an English clergyman or salary for one, continues to perform the service as well as he can." Mr. Tunstall had been appointed, as we have seen, to minister to the English residents of Montreal. At Quebec a more serious change appears to have taken place. No record seems to survive relating how the Bishop threw oil on the troubled waters, but that some arrangement was amicably arrived at, we may assume from the fact that on the arrival of the Bishop, Mr. Montmollin styled himself *Rector of Quebec*, a title assumed by Mr. Toosey on the Bishop's departure.

The Injunctions printed in the *Canadian Magazine* and referred to in the Bishop's letter are as follows:

INJUNCTIONS GIVEN TO THE CLERGY OF THE PROVINCE OF QUEBEC AT THE PRIMARY VISITATION HOLDEN IN THE CITY OF QUEBEC, BY THE RIGHT REVEREND CHARLES, BY DIVINE PERMISSION BISHOP OF NOVA SCOTIA.*

1ST. That the clergy be exemplary in their lives; and that by a diligent discharge of the duties of their functions, they endeavour to promote the spiritual welfare of their respective flocks.

2ND. That in the several ministrations of their office, they do punctually observe the Rubrics contained in the Book of Common Prayer, and the Canons or Ecclesiastical Constitutions published by authority in the year 1603.

3RD. That the clergy in cities do wear their proper habits, on all public occasions, and as often besides as may be convenient; and it is recommended that they, as well as the clergy in the country, do always wear short cassocks, when they do not appear in their habits.

4TH. That every incumbent or officiating clergyman do read divine service twice every Lord's Day, and preach one sermon at least; and it is recommended that in cities and populous districts, two sermons be preached each Lord's Day, namely, one in the forenoon and the other in the afternoon; and also that divine service be read in those places on Wednesdays, Fridays and Holy Days.

---

* I am indebted to W. G. Wurtele, Esq., of Quebec, for the knowledge of these Injunctions.

5TH. That children shall be baptised as the Rubricks direct, on Sundays, in church, or in a place where people assemble for public worship; and that Baptism be not administered in private houses, except in case of necessity, when a child is sick and too weak to be carried abroad.

6TH. That as a practice has prevailed in the western parts of this Province, where no clergymen were settled, for laymen to administer baptism to children, and clergymen to whom these children so baptized were afterwards presented for Baptism have been at a loss how to proceed—it will be advisable in all such cases for the clergy to ask the questions which are set down in the form prescribed for the ministration of Private Baptism, concerning *the person by whom, the matter and form of words*, with which the child was baptized; and if those who bring the child do make such uncertain answers to those questions that it shall appear things were not done according to due order in the above particulars, then let the clergyman baptize the child in the form appointed for public Baptism; saving only that in dipping the child in the font, or pouring water upon it, he shall use this conditional form of words, " If thou art not already baptized,—I baptize thee in the Name of the Father, and of the Son, and of the Holy Ghost."

7TH. That the clergy be very diligent and careful in catechising children and others who shall offer themselves for the purpose every Lord's Day, during the Summer season.

8TH. That the Holy Communion be regularly administered at the three stated Feasts, Christmas, Easter and Whitsunday, in every parish, and as often besides as may be convenient, and it will be advisable to administer the Communion on the first Sunday in every month in the cities of Quebec and Montreal.

9TH. That no fees be asked or demanded for administering either of the Sacraments of Baptism or the Lord's Supper, or for visiting the sick.

10TH. That as the money given at the Offertory should always be applied to charitable purposes, particularly to the relief of poor communicants, and as it may be satisfactory to the parishioners to know how that money is disposed of, it is recommended to each minister to keep an account of the sums collected at the Communion, from time to time, and of the persons among whom it is distributed, and to exhibit the same annually at Easter to the church wardens and vestry.

11TH. That, as it is customary to pay fees for the solemnization of Matrimony, for burying the dead and registering Baptisms, and as it may prevent inconvenience to have the fees for these services ascertained: the clergy may demand ten shillings, equal to two Spanish milled Dollars and no more, for each marriage; the sum of 7s 6d, equal to one Spanish Dollar and a half, and no more, for each funeral, when the Burial Service is read; and one shilling, or one-fifth of a Dollar, and no more, for registering each child that is baptized. And it will be advisable for each clergyman to have the above *Table of Fees* adopted by the church wardens and vestry of his parish.

12TH. That in case an assistant performs any of the above services, and a sum exceeding the stated fee be given for the same, the overplus belongs of right to the assistant.

13TH. That two church wardens, one by the minister and another by the congregation, also two sidesmen or a select vestry, be chosen at Easter, every year in each parish. And it will be advisable for the minister, church wardens, and sidesmen or vestry, to settle the fees for the clerk and sexton, and for a Pall, for digging graves, and for the attendance of a clerk at funerals, with other matters.

14TH. That the clerk be extremely cautious in employing strangers who appear in the character of clergymen to do any duty for them, before they have seen the letters of Orders of such strangers, and are also well satisfied about the regularity of their lives and good moral character.

Done at Quebec this 8th day of August, in the year of our Lord 1789, and in the second year of our consecration.

The remaining part of the article from the *Quebec Gazette* is as follows :

"On Tuesday the following ADDRESS was presented to the Bishop by his clergy :

RIGHT REVEREND SIR,

The scene is now closing upon us, which at once will deprive us of your affectionate care and spiritual assistance. Nor can we without deep regret look upon the season which, tho' the termination of your labours, gives us the first sensations of the greatness of our loss. And who are they that do not sympathize with us ? When look around us we see every one impatient to testify their kindest sentiments of esteem and affection. They reflect with pleasure upon your great affability to all the inhabitants of this country—whilst we cannot but call to mind your condescension and tenderness of regard to your clergy in particular. They seem already actuated with a portion of your spirit, which inspires universal benevolence and zeal for your God—churches already begin to rise—learning and science promise their dawn upon this frozen clime. We hope still to share in the directions which can procure these public benefits, and so far promise ourselves success in the ministry, as we follow our intended Pattern for Imitation. But what reward shall we give for what has been done for us? We commit you to the approbation of your conscience,* and join in recommendation of your welfare to that God whose zealous servant you are. Wishing you a happy return to those who are now stretching out their arms to receive you,

We are, Right Reverend Sir,
With the greatest respect and esteem,
Your most dutiful sons and servants,

DAVID FRANCIS DE MONTMOLLIN,
PHILIP TOOSEY,
DAVID CHS. DELISLE,
JOHN DOTY,
JOHN STUART,
JAMES TUNSTALL,
JOHN LANGHORNE,
L. J. B. N. VEYSSIÈRE.

Quebec, August 10th, 1789."

The Bishop was pleased to return the following answer to this Address:

MY REVEREND BRETHREN,

This affectionate Address at our parting claims my warmest thanks,—be pleased to accept of them—they flow from a heart deeply interested in your welfare, reputation and happiness. My thanks are also due for your kind attention, for your advice and assistance at this visitation.

The approbation which you are pleased to bestow on my endeavours in behalf of religion and literature is very flattering; and I

---

* Were this Address signed by the Swiss clergy only, this clause would perhaps be intelligible.

thank God for any degree of success that those well-meant endeavours may have met with. We are all embarked in the cause of God and His truth—a consciousness of this should animate our exertions, and support us under every obstruction and trial. The Divine Master we serve has set the example of meekness, purity, and love, which we should follow; and whilst we steadfastly copy that pattern, in the discharge of our several duties, we may safely trust the issue to Him, and rest assured of His favour and protection.

I fervently pray the Almighty to direct your conduct, and to prosper your labours : may He dispose the hearts of your respective flocks to profit by these labours, and earnestly to concur with you in what involves their own dearest interests ; thereby alleviating the difficulties of your station, strengthening your hands, and brightening your prospects, so that you may be mutual blessings, and a crown of rejoicing to each other on that awful day when the present scene, with all its delusive objects, shall wholly vanish, and the fate of mankind, according to their conduct here, will be determined for ever.

CHARLES NOVA SCOTIA.

To the issue of the 20th of August we are indebted for the interesting incidents connected with the Bishop's departure from Quebec :

"Sunday last the Right Reverend the Bishop of Nova Scotia preached an excellent farewell sermon at the Recollet church, previous to his leaving this Province, and on Monday at one o'clock in the afternoon, attended by the clergy, citizens, and many of the military gentlemen, he embarked on board His Majesty's *Weasel* Sloop of War, where he was received with a salute of eleven guns, and immediately started for Halifax with a fair wind."

Thus did the first Anglican Episcopal visitation of Canada begin and end. Not only did it add new life and vigour to the Church, but it demonstrated the fact that a Bishop should be appointed to oversee this important country, so rich in natural resources, and so well adapted to become the home of millions of happy people.

CHAPTER VIII.

THE COMPLAINTS AGAINST THE FOREIGN DIVINES.

Probably the most difficult task in the acquisition of accurate knowledge concerning any historical event, is the sifting of evidence. One's judgment is very liable to receive a warp in a certain direction, and to remain under its influence throughout the whole inquiry.

A wrong impression certainly went abroad, soon after the Conquest of Canada, concerning the number of French Protestants in the newly-acquired Province, and there is no doubt that this was partly the cause of the appointment of the Swiss clergy to the first three parishes. A State Paper drawn up in 1786* states that "At the settling of the Peace in 1762 it was represented to Government that there were a vast number of French Protestants in Canada, for whose benefit it would be proper to send out clergymen who could preach in that language, though in reality the number was very small, and the English Protestants were ten times as many."

Canon Hawkins says that Mr. De Montmollin had a few French hearers at Quebec,† "not converts, however, from the Roman Catholics but Huguenots." And the Lutheran Chaplain to the Duke of Brunswick's Dragoon Regiment, Rev. F. V. Melsheimer, made the following entry in his diary‡ on the 29th of May, 1776 :—

"This evening we anchored off the Island of Orleans. It was still early and our captain wanted to go ashore ; he asked me to be of his party, and I, nothing loth, cheerfully jumped into his gig. We found a parish here, with the pastor, a Frenchman by birth and a Protestant by religion. Uprightness and simplicity in all his ways, made this good man of sixty-two a true father to his parishioners, who numbered fifty-four families. These islanders live in noble simplicity. They are nearly all natives and live happily under the British dominion. Their houses are scattered along the shore, each man having his garden and plot of land.........We bought some fresh food and at ten returned on board."

---

* Can. Arch., Series Q, Vol. 49, p. 343.
† Annals of the Diocese of Quebec, page 14.
‡ This document was recently published by the Quebec Literary and Historical Society.

One would naturally arrive at the conclusion that there were French Protestants in considerable numbers in Canada, in the early days of the English regime. Dr. Ogilvie's work at Quebec, the representations on the subject referred to above, and the entry of the Hessian chaplain, would be sufficient, one would think, to establish the fact. But the idea thus gained would be erroneous, for Garneau tells us there were no Huguenots in Canada at the period of the Conquest, and the French Protestants of the Island of Orleans were not emigrants since the Conquest, as they were said to be natives. And the S. P. G. Annual Report states that after Dr. Ogilvie's departure from Quebec in 1763, the French congregations he had gathered together were permitted to dwindle away. Had there been a congregation consisting of fifty-four families on the Island, the clergyman's name would be on the clergy lists and pay rolls, and it would appear year after year in the old *Quebec Almanac*. The Hessian chaplain was probably the victim of a hoax.

A subject of greater consequence to the Church than the alleged disappearance of the French congregation at the Island of Orleans, was the charges brought against the Swiss clergy. This subject absorbed so much attention, and was the cause of so many complaints both to the Government and the Society for the Propagation of the Gospel, that it must now come before us for consideration. Much light has been thrown upon this inquiry in recent years; but it is very necessary to weigh carefully all that bears upon it.

The last semi-official account of some of these charges is that published in the *Annals of the Diocese of Quebec*, by Canon Hawkins, Secretary of the Society for the Propagation of the Gospel. This book was published in 1848. The whole passage is here reproduced :—

" The three next clergymen, of whom we find any mention, seem to have been appointed by the Government under the expectation that an impression might be made upon the French Canadians by clergymen who could perform the Anglican services in the French language. The first was a Monsieur De Montmollin, a Swiss, ordained in our church. His name occurs in the register of Quebec, in the year 1768. He had a few French hearers, not converts, however, for they were all of the old Huguenot stock ; but his imperfect pronunciation marred the effect of his ministrations to the English.

" The second, the Reverend David Chadbrand Delisle, also of

Swiss extraction, and but imperfectly acquainted with our language, was sent by the Government to act in the double capacity of chaplain to the garrison and minister to the English congregation at Montreal.

"Mr. Veyssière, a Recollet friar, who had been disgraced in his own communion, was adopted as the minister at Three Rivers, but seems to have done no more credit to the Church of England than he had done to the Church of Rome."

The authority on which these statements were made was probably the letter of the Reverend Charles Mongan to Colonel Nepean,* which was as follows :—

No. 8, Dufour's Place,
Broad St., Golden Square,
1st Feb., 1786.

Sir,—

From a desire of giving as little interruption as possible, I am induced thus to acquaint you, that, agreeable to your direction, I called upon Dr. Morris (Morice?), with whom, and several others of the principal members of the Society, I have had repeated conversations, and to whom I was happy in being able to give some useful information upon the state of our Church in Canada, having spent a year in that Province, during which time, at the desire of the late Bishop of London, I took every pains to make myself acquainted with that subject, the particulars of which I had the honour of transmitting to his Lordship; but his death happening soon afterwards, prevented those exertions he intended, in showing the Government the necessity of putting our Church upon a more respectable footing in that country, and of sending out ministers to the principal towns who were likely to recover our religion from that state of disrepute into which it had fallen, through the unaccountable neglect of this country in sending out clergymen totally unfit for the situation in which they were placed.

A more particular description of these gentlemen, with a short account of our church affairs in Canada, is contained in the inclosed extracts of a memorial lately transmitted to this country with a hope of obtaining relief.

The Society for Propagating the Gospel seems perfectly convinced of the deplorable state of the Church of England in Canada,

---

* Canadian Archives, Series Q, Vol. 26, page 20.

but the power of redress does not lie with them. They are very willing to contribute their mite towards the support of proper clergymen; but it is with Government alone to make those alterations which are absolutely necessary to the credit and welfare of the Church of England in that country.

From that liberality of mind, and goodness of heart, which mark the character of the worthy nobleman under whose immediate department this subject comes, I feel myself happy in the expectation of that amendment, which the credit of our religion and the happiness of society so loudly call for, and which must not only reflect the highest honour upon his Lordship, but be productive of great political advantage to that part of His Majesty's dominions.

I shall no longer trespass upon your time than to offer my grateful acknowledgments for the civility you have been pleased to honour me with, and to say, that I could have no objection to any preferment in Canada that his Lordship would think proper to place me in.

I have the honour to be, with the greatest respect,
Your most obedient servant,
CHARLES MONGAN.

E. NEPEAN, ESQRE.

The *Extracts from the memorial* referred to in this letter, and which were enclosed in it, were as follows:—*

"*The present state of the Church of England and its Clergy in Canada.*

"At Quebec, the only clergyman of the Church of England is a very old Swedish gentleman who cannot speak one word of plain English—in consequence of which, and his unpopular private conduct, the English inhabitants at Quebec (which are numerous and very respectable) are deprived of Divine Service and the minister an object of contempt and ridicule.

"At Montreal the case is the same—the clergyman is also a foreigner, and speaks English so very unintelligibly that our Church is totally neglected, notwithstanding the English inhabitants here are very numerous and respectable, but not having a proper minister of their own Church are under the necessity of encouraging Presbyterian and other sects, who, taking advantage of the neglected

* Can. Arch., Series Q, Vol. 26, p. 22.

state of our religious affairs in this country, are now crowding in from all quarters of the United States, and, of course, sowing the seeds of that disaffection to our Church and constitution which contributed not a little to the loss of our other colonies.

"At Three Rivers, the situation of our Church is still more unfortunate, and may be justly called *shameful*, for in addition to the inability of the other gentlemen (in the performance of Divine Service with decency and propriety) the clergyman here is that kind of character that would disgrace the meanest profession. He speaks English worse (if possible) than the other two, and was expelled (for some flagitious acts) from a community of Friars to which he belonged, prior to his conversion to our religion.

"This is the true and melancholy state of the Church of England in Canada, and which (if permitted to continue so) it needs no great share of penetration to foresee must soon be followed by the most unhappy political consequences—laying all moral considerations out of the question."

Canon Hawkins was probably unaware that Mr. Mongan's letter was forwarded by Mr. Nepean, on behalf of Lord Sydney, to General Haldimand, late Governor-in-Chief of Canada, for his opinion concerning its contents. General Haldimand's answer bears the date, 8th March, 1786.* He says that the document (*State of Religion*, which was enclosed) was in some parts consistent with truth, but *highly exaggerated*. No such unhappy political consequences had followed as were reported, the so-called "New England emissaries" being loyalist clergymen driven from their possessions. Mr. Stuart is distinguished for his active, useful, exertions in the royal cause, the other two were indigent and not in the least dangerous. The following entry was made the same day by the General in his private Diary.†

"Received this morning a letter from Mr. Nepean enclosing a letter respecting the state of the Protestant Clergy in Canada, and asking on behalf of Lord Sydney my opinion thereon, as his Lordship wished to give no reply before knowing what I thought of it. I answered that whilst there might be some truth in the memorial, it was extremely exaggerated; that I had left affairs in that country

---

* Can. Arch., Series Q, Vol. 26-1, p. 62.
† Canadian Archives, Series B, Vol. 230-2. Wednesday, 8th March, 1786.

as I had found them, and that my feeling was that it would be more suitable to send it to Brigadier Hope to obtain information, etc., etc. I was much surprised that having been here for more than a year, during which nothing has ever been communicated to me, they should wish to consult me now, no doubt in order to throw on me the responsibility for all the changes it is proposed to make. Besides, I believe that this memorial has been drawn up by the minister Dauté (Doty) with the advice and assistance of Hamilton and Caldwell."

No definite charges were brought against Mr. Delisle and Mr. DeMontmollin, and the worst that was said of Veyssière was his alleged expulsion from the Order of the Recollets. But that was an imaginary offence, one entirely disproved by the Provincial Commissary of the Order, Père Emmanuel Crespel, himself, who asserted, as we have seen, that Mr. Veyssière was "a man of very good behaviour, and exact in all his duties"; and also by Mr. Veyssière's own card of thanks to his late superior. I can only learn from Roman Catholic sources at Three Rivers that there are no charges against his moral character, that to his ambition alone is ascribed his defection from the Church of Rome, and the only comfort his confrères derived from his action was the somewhat grim consolation that his second marriage was a very unhappy one.

The other personal charges against Veyssière whilst pastor of Three Rivers are altogether of a general character. The paper we have read on the Canadian clergy of the period styled his conduct as "shameful, such as would disgrace the meanest profession." The first Bishop of Nova Scotia in 1789 reported to the S.P.G. that Mr. Veyssière "does us no credit, and is almost useless as a clergyman"; and the first Bishop of Quebec, in the report to the Colonial office of his first visitation of the Diocese, described him as "a bad character." Had there been anything against his moral character, the Bishops would have silenced him, but they did not do so. Dr. Inglis found him "incompetent to read and preach in English, but for want of an English clergyman or salary for one, continues to perform the service as well as he can."* And Dr. Mountain appoints his brother, Dr. Jehoshaphat Mountain, as his assistant.†

---

* Can. Arch., Series Q, Vol. 2, page 678.
† Do., Vol. 69-2, page 385.

84   *The Church of England in Canada.*

A general charge was brought against these clergymen that they performed little or no duty. The following extracts are from a State Paper also drawn up in 1786.*

" The neglect of church duty appears from repeated accounts sent to the Bishop of London, and the Society, to be most shameful.

" There is not a single Protestant Church in the whole Province.

" The French minister at Quebec, a reformed Jesuit,† cannot preach in English, and is very negligent in his duty.

" The minister of Trois Rivières is a most dissolute character. He was formerly a Recollet monk at that place, quarrelled with his Abbot, and then got ordained here in England,‡ and went back the Protestant minister of that place, where he never does any duty at all.

" The minister at Montreal (who is also chaplain of the garrison), when he does officiate, it is in the Chapel of the Recollets Convent, on Sunday mornings only, and on Christmas day and Good Friday.

" The paucity of French hearers hath so far set aside divine service and preaching in French, that the Society have credible information that for four years together not four sermons were preached in that language. The evening service is never performed, and the Sacrament of the Lord's Supper not administered above three or four times in a year at Montreal, not so often at Quebec, and not at all at Trois Rivières."§

As the terms of their commissions bound the clergy to perform Divine Services in those buildings which the Government was to provide for the purpose, and the Government made arrangements for services of an hour's duration on Sunday mornings only, the Government, at any rate, could not entertain seriously the complaint that the pastors would not read the Evening Prayer,—the obvious answer being, " If you are not satisfied with the arrangements the Government has made, it is your duty to provide for this and other

---

* Canadian Archives, Series Q, Vol. 49, pages 343-353.

† Mr. DeMontmollin was never a Roman Catholic.

‡ Mr. Veyssière, being in Roman Orders, was not re-ordained. The Episcopal Register of the Diocese of London has been carefully examined, through the kindness of the Lord Bishop, with the result that no such ordination took place.

§ Sir Frederick Haldimand's belief that the Rev. John Doty was the author of the State Paper forwarded for his inspection is strengthened by a perusal of Mr. Doty's Report to the S. P. G., in January, 1783, and printed in full in Pascoe's *Digest of S. P. G. Records*, p. 140, in which whole paragraphs are identical with those contained in the two papers of 1786.

services yourselves." As a matter of fact the Government was always urging the people, even in garrison towns, to make provision for their own spiritual wants—the annual grants towards clerical stipends, the enactments concerning rectories, and the setting aside of land for clergy reserves, were all intended as inducements to self-help and self-support. One of the most serious complaints was that the Holy Communion was not celebrated at Montreal more than three or four times a year—a misfortune, however, that was not confined to Canada, as some of the largest London churches were open to the same charge. This complaint appears to have originated in the Report of Rev. John Doty to the Society in 1783, where the same statement is made, that "the Sacrament of the Lord's Supper is administered not above three or four times in a year at Montreal, not so often at Quebec, and not at all at Trois Rivières." This statement could not have been based on any definite knowledge, as Dr. Mountain, we are expressly informed, increased the communicants' roll at Three Rivers from four to eighteen. There must, therefore, have been celebrations sometimes. Mr. Doty's Report was drawn up in January, 1783. It is somewhat remarkable that on the 14th of February, in the same year, there should have been a memorial presented to the Government by the British residents of Three Rivers,* praying that that part of the Recollet church hitherto used as a store for medicines be transferred to the Rev. Mr. Veyssière for public worship. Attention must be drawn to the fact that at no time was his removal requested; and here was a petition for a larger place for worship, the court room being found too small to accommodate the numbers attending divine service. Turning to the evidence afforded by the parish registers, I find that they exhibit a constant array of entries during the entire period. The Montreal Register contains 1298 entries of Births, Marriages and Deaths, among the British residents, between the years 1766 and 1787; that of Three Rivers, 405 between 1768 and 1793; whilst the Quebec Register contains probably twice as many entries as the Registers of Montreal and Three Rivers combined.

But whatever may fairly be urged in justification of the Swiss clergy, it must be remembered that during their entire pastorate, the Church made no progress among the British residents, but was

---

*Canadian Archives, Series B, Vol. 217, p. 307.

terribly hampered by their incapacity. They "stuck to their post" like grim death, it is true; but "dying in harness," said the late Bishop Williams of Quebec, in a speech at the Diocesan Synod, " however the phrase may gratify one's sense of faithfulness to the Church, very often means the death of the parish." Never was this wise remark more painfully illustrated than in the case before us. The dog-in-the-manger principle is especially a dangerous one, and, whether it proceed from inability to be "understanded of the people," from being "understanded" too well, or from any other infirmity whatever, it is always detrimental to the best interests of the Church.

CHAPTER IX.

THE CLERGY LIST OF 1790.

THE visit of the Bishop of Nova Scotia to Canada, being the first opportunity the Church in this Province had of seeing itself properly equipped and presented before the people, marks a favourable opportunity for taking a brief survey of the position the Church occupied in the country.

A State Paper drawn up in the year 1786* presents so many interesting points that I make a few extracts from it.

"Three clergymen with a stipend each of £200 a year, were sent out to their respective Parishes of Quebec, Montreal and Trois Rivières, viz.: Mr. DeMontmollin, Mr. Delisle and Mr. Veyssière. About 6 years ago, a Mr. Geary went over for one winter, with the same salary, but came back to England. And last year, the Revd. Mr. Toosey, who has two Livings in Suffolk, was sent in his room, without being appointed to any settled place wherein to officiate as a clergyman. These are all the clergy in that extensive Province, except the Rev. Mr. Stuart and Mr. Doty, the Society's Missionaries; lately placed, the one at Cataraqui, and the other at Sorrell, with a salary of £50 a year from the Society..........A Missionary is wanted also at Johnstown (Cornwall). 36 miles above Coteau de Lac, with the assistance of Government.....There are 44 families of the Church settled at Oswegatchie, where a Mr. John Bryan at present officiates."
The same paper contains the following list, although drawn up in 1790:—

Episcopal or English Church.

	Salaries.
Mr. DeLisle, Montreal	£200
Tunstall	100
De Montmollin, Quebec	200
Toosey	200
Veyssière, Three Rivers	200
Doty, William Henry	100
Stuart, Kingston	100

* Canadian Archives, Series Q, Vol. 49, page 343.

88   The Church of England in Canada.

Mr. Bryan, Cornwall.. 50
Langhorne—near Kingston, Miss : from Ye Society for
propagating Ye Gospel with £50 and from Government £100.. 150

Church of Scotland.

Messrs. Henry & Spark, Quebec, Bethune near Oswegatchie... 50

                                                                         ─────
                                                                         £1,350

The following paper is most important :
A List of all the Protestant Clergy in the Province of Quebec, with their place of residence, salaries from the Crown, etc.[*]

The Revd. Philip Toosey, Ecclesiastical Commissary of the Eastern District of Canada, to which no salary is as yet annexed. The same person ministers to the English congregation in Quebec. Salary from the Crown, £200 sterling per annum.

In Quebec, the Capital of the British Empire in America, there is no Church belonging to the English congregation, no Parsonage House, Glebe Land, Tythe, or pecuniary composition, as yet assigned to the Minister.

The Revd. William Aked, Chaplain to the garrison of Quebec—Salary £115.5 stg. per ann. He neither resides, nor pays for his duty being done, but is much wanted for his garrison duty, to assist in the service of the Church, and to be ready in case of any ill, or any other avocation.

The Revd. Francis David De Montmollin, appointed to read and preach in French. Salary £200 stg. per annum. Not being found competent by the Bishop of Nova Scotia to read and preach in English, he does no duty, there being no Canadian Protestants to form a congregation.

MONTREAL. The Reverend David Chadbrand Delisle, appointed to read and preach in French at Montreal, and being found incompetent by the Bishop of Nova Scotia to read and preach in English, he does no duty, there being no Canadian Protestants to form a congregation. Salary £200 stg. per annum. The same person chaplain to the garrison of Montreal. Salary £115.5 stg. per annum.

The Revd. James Tunstall, appointed by the Bishop of Nova Scotia assistant minister at Montreal, salary £100 stg. per annum.

─────────

[*] Canadian Archives, Series Q, Vol. 2, page 678.

There is a Church for the use of the English Congregation, but no Parsonage-House, or Glebe-Land as yet assigned to the minister.

THREE RIVERS. The Revd. John Baptist Veyssière, settled at Three Rivers, to read and preach in French, found incompetent by the Bishop of Nova Scotia to read and preach in English, but for want of an English Clergyman, or salary for one, continues to perform the services as well as he can. Salary £200 stg. per annum. There is neither Parsonage House nor Glebe Land.

WILLIAM HENRY. The Revd. John Doty, minister of William Henry (late Sorel). Salary £100 stg. per annum. There is a Church, but no Parsonage House or Glebe Land.

WESTERN DISTRICT. The Revd. John Stuart, Ecclesiastical Commissary of the Western District of Canada, to which no salary is as yet annexed. The same person minister of Kingston (late Cataraqui). Salary £100 stg. per annum. There is a Glebe, but no Parsonage House yet built.

ERNEST TOWN. The Revd. John Langham (Langhorne), minister of Ernest Town. Salary £100 stg. per annum. There is a Glebe, but no Parsonage House yet built.

The above are all the Protestant Clergy in the extensive Province of Quebec, which is thickly settled in many places with Loyal Protestant inhabitants, anxiously praying that Ministers may be settled in their respective Parishes.

English Clergy, 6. Sum total of their salaries...... £715.05.
French Clergy, 3.   Sum total of their salaries......   715.05.

£1430.10.

Quebec, October 28th, 1790.

PHILIP TOOSEY,

{ Ecclesiastical Commissary of the
  Eastern District of Canada.

The Right Honorable
   Guy, Lord Dorchester.

If the Commissary's list contains the names of all the Anglican Clergy in the Province, as he asserts, then Mr. Bryan of Cornwall must have died, or possibly removed from the country during the summer of 1790. I have found very little information concerning his life and work at Cornwall. Canon Pettit writes on this subject:

"I never heard of the Rev. Mr. Bryan until this Spring (1892), when, after the funeral of a very old woman belonging to one of the old families — a Mrs. Smith — a paper was found among the old documents in the house, signed by ' John Smith and John Pescod, church wardens ' which was a brief contract entered into by them to build a house for the Rev. Mr. Bryan...... This contract was drawn up in 1788." Among the *Minutes of Council and Miscellaneous Correspondence** for the first half of the year 1790, are some *Remarks on New Johnstown* (*Cornwall*), in which is given a list of settlers holding " large tracts which are fenced round in the heart of the town, and the streets are included in these enclosures." This list contains the name of the Revd. Mr. Bryan, and reports him as occupying twelve acres of land.

---

* Can. Arch., Series Q, Vol. 45-2, pp. 436-9.

CHAPTER X.

THE CONSTITUTIONAL ACT OF 1791.

At the Conquest, whilst the Roman Catholic Church was wisely tolerated, and as a matter of fact left in possession of her property, excepting only the Jesuits and Recollets, it was distinctly understood in the Imperial Parliament that the Anglican Establishment was to be the National Church.

But various difficulties hindered the successful accomplishment of this scheme. One of the chief of these was the Quebec Act of 1774, which, by granting to the Roman Catholic Church the legal right to collect tithes, practically established that Church, and set up a very powerful rival in the Province. But even in that Act provision was made for the "encouragement of the Protestant religion, and for the maintenance and support of a Protestant clergy." The Government of the day knew but one Protestant religion and clergy, as is manifested by the instructions issued to the Governors. Thus the parishes of Quebec, Montreal, and Three Rivers had been established soon after the Conquest, and they were supported to the extent of £200 each, annually, whilst only an occasional grant of £50 was made to other Protestant bodies. It was not until 1794 that the Presbyterian ministers at Montreal and Quebec were granted each an annual allowance of £50. On the 31st of December, 1793, Lord Dorchester recommended that "a discretionary power be given to allow the Dissenting ministers at Quebec and Montreal £50 a year each, so long as their conduct is such as becomes good and loyal subjects."* The Governor's request was granted, confined, however, to the Presbyterian ministers only.† Had the Government used the word *Protestant* in the broad sense as subsequently interpreted, and had the various Protestant bodies so understood it in the early days, then equal support with the Church of England would have been demanded as a right, and the Church of Scotland would not have been content to receive

---
* Can. Archives, Series Q, Vol. 67, p. 67.
† Do., p. 17.

the mere pittance allowed her, and to have this doled out to her as a dissenting body.

The United Empire Loyalists were instrumental in effecting a great change. In compliance with their repeated demands the Constitutional Act of 1791 was conceded. In truth, the religious clauses of this Act are little more than an enlargement of the provision for the *Protestant Religion* in the Quebec Act, only such important privileges were added as seemingly to justify the assertion that this Act virtually repealed the former. By this Act Rectories were to be established throughout the country on the same legal footing as the Rectories in England, excepting that in lieu of endowments and tithes, a special grant of one-seventh of all the unconceded lands in the Province was made for the support of the clergy, all of whom were under canonical obedience to the Lord Bishop of Nova Scotia.

The chief clauses of this Act, so far as it bears on the Church of England, are as follows :

XXXV. And whereas, by the above mentioned Act,* passed in the fourteenth year of the Reign of his present majesty, it was declared, that the Clergy of the Church of Rome, in the Province of Quebec, might hold, receive and enjoy their accustomed dues and rights, with respect to such persons only as should profess the said religion; provided nevertheless, that it should be lawful for his Majesty, his heirs or successors, to make such provision out of the rest of the said accustomed dues and rights, for the encouragement of the *Protestant Religion*, and for the maintenance and support of a *Protestant Clergy* within the said Province, as he or they should from time to time think necessary and expedient, and whereas by his Majesty's Royal instructions, given under his Majesty's royal sign manual on the 3rd day of January, in the year of Our Lord one thousand seven hundred and seventy-five, to Guy Carleton, Esqre., now Lord Dorchester, at that time his Majesty's Captain General and Governor-in-chief, in and over his Majesty's Province of *Quebec*, his Majesty was pleased, amongst other things, to direct, " That no incumbent professing the religion of the Church of *Rome*, appointed to any Parish in the said Province, should be entitled to receive any tithes for lands or possessions occupied by a Protestant, but that such tithes should be received by such persons as the said said Guy Carle-

---

* The Quebec Act of 1774.

The Constitutional Act of 1791. 93

ton, Esqre,... should appoint, and should be reserved in the hands of his Majesty's Receiver-General of the said Province, for the support of a *Protestant Clergy* in his Majesty's said Province, to be actually resident within the same, and not otherwise, according to such directions as the said *Guy Carleton, Esqre*, his Majesty's Captain General, etc... should receive from his Majesty in that behalf: and that in like manner all growing rents and profits of a vacant benefice should, during such vacancy, be reserved for, and applied to, the like uses ;" And whereas his Majesty's pleasure has likewise been signified to the same effect in his Majesty's Royal Instructions, given in like manner to Sir Frederick Haldimand, Knight of the most honourable Order of the Bath, late his Majesty's Captain-General and Governor-in-chief, in and over his Majesty's said Province of Quebec... etc., shall remain and continue to be in full force and effect in each of the said two *Provinces of Upper Canada and Lower Canada*, respectively, in so far as the said Declaration or Provisions respectively, or any part thereof, shall be expressly varied or repealed by any Act or Acts which may be passed by the Legislative Council and Assembly of the said Provinces respectively, and assented to by his Majesty, his heirs or successors, under the restrictions hereinafter provided.

XXXVI. And whereas his Majesty has been graciously pleased, by message to both Houses of Parliament, to express his Royal Desire to be enabled to make "a permanent appropriation of Lands "in the said Provinces, for the support and maintenance of a "Protestant Clergy within the same, in proportion to such lands as "have been already granted within the same by his Majesty ....
"Therefore, for the purpose of more effectually fulfilling his Majesty's "gracious intention as aforesaid, and of providing for the due exe-"cution of the same in all time to come, be it enacted by the "authority aforesaid, That it shall and may be lawful for his Majesty, "his heirs or successors, to authorise the Governor or Lieutenant of "each of the said Provinces respectively or the person administer-"ing the government therein, to make from and out of the lands of "the Crown within such Province, such allotment and appropriation "of lands, for the support and maintenance of a Protestant Clergy "within the same, as may bear a due proportion to the amount of "such lands within the same as have at any time been granted by "or under the authority of his Majesty.........and it shall be, as "nearly as the same can be estimated at the time of making such

" grant, equal in value to the seventh part of the lands so granted.
" ....And that whenever any grant of Lands within either of the
" said Provinces shall hereafter be made by, or under the authority
" of His Majesty (or his Successors, &c.), there shall, at the same
" time, be made in respect of the same, a proportionable allotment
" and appropriation of Lands (one seventh) for the above mentioned
" purpose, within the Township or Parish to which such Lands so
" to be granted shall appertain, or be annexed, or as nearly adjacent
" thereto as circumstances will admit; and that no such Grants
" shall be valid or effectual, unless the same shall contain a specifi-
" cation of the Lands so allotted and appropriated, in respect of the
" Lands to be thereby granted; and that such Lands so to be
" appropriated, shall be as nearly as the nature of the case will per-
" mit, of like quality as the Lands in respect of which the same are
" so allotted, and shall be as nearly as the same can be estimated at
" the time of making such Grant, equal in value to the seventh part
" of the Lands so granted."

XXXVII. And be it further enacted by the Authority aforesaid, That all and every the rents, profits or emoluments, which may at any time arise from such lands so allotted and appropriated as aforesaid, shall be applicable solely to the maintenance and support of a Protestant clergy within the Province in which the same shall be situated, and to no other use or purpose whatever.

XXXVIII. ....That it should and might be lawful for His Majesty, his heirs or successors, to authorize the Governor or Lieutenant-Governor of each of the said Provinces respectively, or the person administering the Government therein from time to time with the advice of such Executive Council as should have been appointed by His Majesty, his heirs or successors, within such Province for the affairs thereof, to constitute and erect within every Township or Parish which then was or thereafter might be formed, constituted or erected within such Province one or more Parsonage or Rectory or Parsonages or Rectories according to the Establishment of the Church of England; and from time to time by an Instrument under the Great Seal of such Province to endow every such Parsonage or Rectory with so much or such part of the lands so allotted and appropriated as aforesaid in respect of any lands within such Township or Parish which should have been granted subsequent to the commencement of the said Act, or of such lands as might have been allotted and appropriated for the same purpose

The Constitutional Act of 1791. 95

by or in virtue of any instruction which might be given by His Majesty in respect of any lands granted by His Majesty before the commencement of the said Act, as such Governor, Lieutenant-Governor, or person administering the Government should, with the advice of the said Executive Council, judge to be expedient under the then existing circumstances of such Township or Parish.

XXXIX. Limits the persons to be presented to such Parsonages or Rectories as follows :—"An Incumbent or Minister of the Church of England, who shall have been duly ordained according to the Rites of the said Church, such persons to hold and enjoy the same as fully and amply and in the same manner, and on the same terms and conditions, and liable to the performance of same duties, as an Incumbent of a Benefice or Cure in England."

XL. Renders these Clergy subject and liable to all rights of Institution, and all other spiritual and Ecclesiastical Authority of the Bishop of Nova Scotia, or such other Authority as may hereafter be lawfully granted by His Majesty, within the said Provinces, or either of them respectively, according to the Laws and Canons of the Church of England—which are legally established and received in England.

XLI. Provided always, and be it further enacted by the authority aforesaid, That the several provisions herein-before contained respecting the allotment and appropriation of lands for the support of a Protestant Clergy within the said Provinces, and also respecting the constituting, erecting and endowing parsonages or rectories within the said Provinces, and also respecting the presentation of Incumbents or ministers to the same, and also respecting the manner in which such incumbents or ministers shall hold and enjoy the same, and shall be subject to be varied or repealed by any express provisions for that purpose, contained in any Act or Acts which may be passed by the Legislative Councils and Assembly of the said Provinces respectively, and assented to by his Majesty, his heirs or successors, under the restriction hereinafter provided.

XLII. ....That it shall not be lawful for His Majesty, his heirs or successors, to signify his or their assent to any such Act or Acts, until thirty days after the same shall have been laid before the two Houses of the Imperial Parliament—or to assent to any such Act or Acts, in case either House of Parliament shall, within the said thirty days, address His Majesty, his heirs or successors, to withhold his or their assent. And no such Act shall be valid or effectual to the purposes of any such change within either of the said Provinces, unless the Legislative Council and Assembly of such Province shall, in the Session in which the same shall have been passed by them, have presented to the Governor or, &c., an address or addresses specifying that such Act contains provisions for some of the said purposes herein before specially described, and desiring that, in order to give effect to the same, such Act should be transmitted without delay, for the purpose of being laid before Parliament previous to the signification of His Majesty's assent thereto.

The meaning of this Act was for more than half a century fiercely disputed by other religious bodies who claimed as *Protestants* a share of the Clergy reserves, although no clergymen, except those of the Church of England, *could* by any construction satisfy the 38th, 39th and 40th clauses, and none others *would* submit to the spiritual jurisdiction established by the 40th clause of the Act. Yet the Act of 1854 was adverse to the Church's claim.

One clergyman came to labour in the newly organized Province of Upper Canada between the passing of this Act and the establishment of the See of Quebec, and it is a pleasure to recall his life and work.

Rev. Robert Addison was born in England in the year 1754 The following personal notes are taken from a paper read by the Revd. Dr. Scadding at the Centenary Celebration of St. Mark's Church, Niagara, on the 11th of July, 1892 :—

" Mr. Addison was a graduate of Trinity College, Cambridge, taking his degree of M.A. in 1785. We have thus to imagine him often traversing the grand quadrangle of Henry the Eighth's famous foundation, and passing in and out familiarly among door-ways and chambers teeming with memories of Lord Bacon, George Herbert, Robert Nelson, Sir Isaac Newton, and the other innumerable historic worthies, who have been members of Trinity. His surroundings at Cambridge were doubtless congenial to his character ; and I have been assured that Bishop Watson, of Llandaff, the well-known author of the " Apology," had said that the English Church was losing a scholar of no ordinary quality, when, in 1792, Mr. Addison decided to make far-off Canada the scene of his ministrations. His prospects at home were bright ; to be a member of Trinity College, Cambridge, gave a prestige to a man everywhere in England, and this determination on the part of Mr. Addison was plainly an act of unselfishness. The national Church was calling on her sons personally to assist her in fulfilling her duty towards the wide domain brought within her jurisdiction through the acquisition of Canada. He felt himself impelled to obey that call. The English Church was fortunate in having so worthy a representative in these parts at so early a period."

On Mr. Addison's arrival at Niagara or Newark, as it was then called, he opened a school, the first established in that part of the world, and it is satisfactory to record its successful operation for many years. His parish register dates back to the 9th of July, 1792.

Two months after Mr. Addison's appointment at Niagara took effect, a paper was drawn up by Mr. Richard Cartwright on the facilities for solemnizing marriages in the Upper Province, and on the state of the Church of England in the same regions. This was drawn up in view of the proposal to establish a Canadian Bishopric. The document is here given in full.

Report on the subject of Marriages and the state of the Church of England in the Province of Upper Canada, humbly submitted to His Excellency Governor Simcoe.*

The Country now Upper Canada was not settled or cultivated in any part except the settlement of Detroit, till the year one thousand seven hundred and eighty-four, when the several Provincial Corps doing Duty in the Province of Quebec were reduced, and together with many Loyalists from New-York, established in different parts of this Province, chiefly along the River St. Lawrence and the Bay of Quenti. In the meanwhile from the year 1777 many families of the Loyalists belonging to Butler's Rangers, the Royal Yorkers, Indian Department and other corps doing Duty at the Upper Posts, had from Time to time come into the country, and many young women of these families were contracted in marriage, which could not be regularly solemnized, there being no Clergyman at the Posts, nor in the whole country between them and Montreal. The practice in such cases usually was to go before the officer commanding the Post, who publickly read to the parties the Matrimonial Service in the Book of Common Prayer, using the Ring and observing the other forms there prescribed, or if he declined it, as was sometimes the case, it was done by the Adjutants of the Regiment. After the settlements were formed in 1784, the Justices of

* Canadian Archives, Series Q, Vol. 279-1, page 174.

the Peace used to perform the Marriage Ceremony till the establishment of Clergymen in the Country, when this practice adopted only from necessity hath been discontinued in the Districts where Clergymen reside.

This is not yet the case with them all; for though the two lower Districts have had each of them a Protestant clergyman since the year 1786;* it is but a few months since this (Nassau or Home) District hath been provided with one†; and the Western District in which the settlement of Detroit is included, is to this Day destitute of that useful and respectable Order of men; Yet the Town of Detroit is and has been since the conquest of Canada inhabited for the most part by Traders of the Protestant Religion who reside there with their families, and among whom Intermarriages have taken place, which formerly were solemnized by the Commanding officer, or some other Layman occasionally appointed by the inhabitants for reading prayers to them on Sundays, but of late more commonly by the Magistrates since Magistrates have been appointed for that District.

From these circumstances it has happened that the Marriages of the generality of the inhabitants of Upper Canada are not valid in Law, and that their children must *stricto jure* be considered as il'egitimate, and consequently not intitled to inherit their property. Indeed this would have been the case, in my opinion, had the Marriage Ceremony been performed even by a regular Clergyman, and with due observance of all the Forms prescribed by the Laws of England. For the clause in the Act of the 14th year of His Present Majesty for regulating the Government of Quebec which declares, " That in all cases of controversy relative to property and Civil Rights, resort shall be had to the Laws of Canada as the Rule for the Decision of the same," appears to me to invalidate all Marriages not solemnized according to the Rites of the Church of Rome, so far as these Marriages are considered as giving any title to property.‡

---

* Reference to the map shows that these two lower Districts of Upper Canada contained Oswegatchie and Cataraqui.

† Mr. Addison.

‡ Mr. Cartwright seems strangely enough to have overlooked the fact that the provisions of this 8th clause of the Act are confined exclusively to " His Majesty's Canadian subjects within the Province of Quebec, the religious Orders and Communities only excepted." For His Majesty's English subjects in Canada, special provision was made in the 6th clause of the same Act, " For the maintenance and support of a Protestant clergy." The Government can scarcely be charged with the appointment of clergymen to cures in Canada, and at the same time by special enactment making their official acts illegal.

Such being the case, it is obvious that it requires the Interposition of the Legislature as well to settle what is past, as to provide some Regulations for the future, in framing of which it should be considered that good policy requires that in a new Country at least, matrimonial connections should be made as easy as may be consistent with the Importance of such Engagements ; and having pledged myself to bring this Business forward early in the next Session, I am led to hope that your Excellency will make such Representations to His Majesty's Ministers as will induce them to consent to such arrangements respecting this Business as the circumstances of the Country may render expedient, Measures for this purpose having been postponed only because they might be thought to interfere with their Views respecting the Clergy of the Establishment.

Of this Church I am myself a Member, and am sorry to say that the State of it in this Province is not very flattering. A very small proportion of the Inhabitants of Upper Canada have been educated in this Persuasion, and the Emigrants to be expected from the United States will for the most part be Sectaries or Dissenters ; and nothing prevents the Teachers of this class from being proportionally numerous, but the Inability of the People at present to provide for their support. In the Eastern District, the most populous part of the Province, there is no Church Clergyman. They have a Presbyterian Minister, formerly Chaplain to the 84th Regiment, who receives from Government fifty Pounds p. ann. They have also a Lutheran Minister who is supported by his Congregation, and the Roman Catholic Priest settled at St. Regis occasionally officiates for the Scots Highlanders settled in the lower part of the District, who are very numerous and all Catholics. There are also many Dutch Calvinists in this part of the Province who have made several attempts to get a Teacher of their own Sect, but hitherto without success.*

In the Midland District, where the members of the Church are more numerous than in any other part of the Province, there are

---

* We learn from this paper that no one had yet succeeded Mr. Bryan, and that Mr. Bethune (Presbyterian) was still officiating in the District.
The first Bishop of Quebec, in the autumn of 1794, brought the spiritual destitution of the settlers between Montreal and Kingston very forcibly to the notice of the Government. From Montreal to Kingston there was not, he said, one Protestant Church or place of worship, except one Lutheran chapel, and one, perhaps two, Presbyterian. The instruction is limited to these small congregations, or to those reached by itinerating Methodists. From Montreal to Baudet (about 50 miles), there were six Roman Catholic churches. From that point to Kingston, the inhabitants, with the exception of a few Scotch Romanists, are all Protestants. Can. Arch., Series Q, Vol. 69-2, pp. 385-404.

two Church Clergymen* who are allowed one hundred pounds stg. p. ann. each by Government, and fifty pounds each by the Society for the Propagation of the Gospel. There are here also some itinerant Methodist Preachers, the Followers of whom are numerous. And many of the Inhabitants of the greatest property are Dutch Calvinists, who have for some time past been using their endeavours to get a Minister of their own Sect among them.

In the Home District there is one clergyman who hath been settled here since the month of July last.† The Scots Presbyterians, who are pretty numerous here, and to which Sect the most respectable part of the Inhabitants belong, have built a Meeting House, and raised a Subscription for a Minister of their own who is shortly expected among them. There are here also many Methodists and Dutch Calvinists.

In the Western District there are no other clergy than those of the Church of Rome. The Protestant Inhabitants here are principally Presbyterians.

From this Statement your Excellency will be able to draw the proper Conclusions; and to judge how far the establishing the Hierarchy of the Church of England in this Province may be proper and expedient.

I have the Honor to be,
With the most profound Respect,
Your Excellency's
Most humble servant,
RICHD. CARTWRIGHT, jun.

Newark, 12th October, 1792.

In forwarding Mr. Cartwright's Report to the Colonial office, accompanied by Chief Justice Osgoode's Upper Canadian Marriage Bill, Governor Simcoe anxiously called the attention of the Ministry to the ecclesiastical state of the Province, and especially to the Church which cannot be established owing to the want of a Bishop.‡ The distance of the Bishop of Nova Scotia, he says, renders it less practicable to resort to him than to the Bishops of England and Ireland, and on the other hand those ordained by United States Bishops are incapacitated from doing duty in Upper Canada. An opportunity is thus given for the introduction of sectaries hostile to the British Constitution.

---

* Messrs. Stuart and Langhorne.
† Mr. Addison.
‡ Canadian Archives, Series Q, Vol. 279-1, p. 169.

CHAPTER XI.

THE EPISCOPAL APPOINTMENT.

THE first name that appears to have been brought forward in connection with the Bishopric of Quebec was that of the Rev. Samuel Peters, D.D. He was the son of John Peters, of Hebron, Connecticut, whose name is prominent in the *Hebron Land Records*, vol. IX, p. 264, as conveying to the S. P. G. about 30 acres of land for a glebe for the Church of England, and which came into the possession of the Parish of St. Peter's Church in that town as the legal successor of the Church of England there. This land was leased by the Parish on the 25th of May, 1795, to S. W. Case for the full term of 9999 years—he " paying therefor yearly during the said term, unto us, John Sutton and John T. Peters, church wardens of said society, and to our successors in said office, the annual rent of one grain of pure silver, or other silver or gold equivalent (if demanded), upon the festival of St. John the Baptist, in each year ensuing the date of these presents, during the term above said."* Samuel Peters was born in the year 1735,† graduated at Yale College, was ordained in England, and eventually inducted into the Parish of Hebron in 1758.‡

This parish had for twenty years been striving to obtain a clergyman. "People must have been truly 'athirst for God,'" says the S. P. G. Record (page 841), "who could—as the inhabitants of Hebron in Connecticut did for twenty years—persevere and at great expense, in sending to England four candidates successively, before they succeeded in obtaining a resident Missionary. The first of these candidates, Mr. Dean (1745), perished at sea while returning. The next, Mr. Colton, died of small-pox within a week after his return (1752). The third, Mr. Usher, was on the return voyage taken prisoner by the French (1757), and died in the Castle of Bayonne of small-pox. The last, Mr. Peters, was taken ill with the same disease in England, but recovered and returned, to the joy of his flock."

Mr. Peters continued in the charge of this Parish until the outbreak of the Revolutionary War, when in 1774 he "left his mission

---

* See the *Living Church*, Aug. 5, 1893. † Sabine's Loyalists, p. 181.
‡ S. P. G. Records, p. 853.

to avoid the fury of an outrageous multitude, who, after the most inhuman treatment of him, still threatened his life."*

Thenceforth Mr. Peters became a refugee in England.†

He is supposed to have been a resident of Canada for a few years, but does not seem to have had any spiritual charge in the country, and his name does not figure in the usual clergy lists. Mr. Peters was the candidate favoured by Governor Simcoe, the first Lieutenant Governor of Upper Canada, and must have been possessed of excellent qualifications to have enjoyed his friendship, and to have received his strong recommendations for so exalted a position.

The proposal of Mr. Peters for the office was made by Governor Simcoe in a letter to the Colonial Office, dated from London, June 2, 1791.‡ He declares that it is "indispensable that a Bishop should be appointed for Upper Canada." He has, he says, strongly recommended Mr. Peters, late of Connecticut, as a proper person for the Episcopal functions. Should the appointment be made, Mr. Peters would go back to Connecticut for the purpose of inviting the loyal clergymen of the Church of England, or those Puritans who would embrace the doctrines of the Church, to settle with their parishioners and others, in the proposed capital.

The interest felt by Governor Simcoe in the establishment of a Canadian See, and especially in the appointment of Mr. Peters, is shown in a subsequent letter to Dundas,§ in which he makes the practical offer to forego £500 a year of his own income towards the Episcopal stipend, in case the appointment of a Bishop for Canada is withheld on account of the expense.

There is a letter from Samuel Peters to Lord Grenville, dated Pimlico, 19th November, 1791, stating that his friends in America desire to know, if possible, not later than January, whether he will be appointed to the proposed See, and go out as Bishop of Canada. If the appointment is made, he suggests an early arrangement to enable him to reach Upper Canada before the snow and ice disappear the following spring. February and March are the best months for travelling on the snow.|| There are several letters written by Mr. Peters, but as they are connected with political matters, or

---

* S. P. G. Records, p. 48.
† Do., 853.
‡ Canadian Archives, Series Q, Vol. 278, p. 228.
§ Do., Vol. 57-1, p. 176.
|| Do., Vol. 57-1, p. 197.

relate wholly to the Treasury Department, they need not be particularly referred to. The last of these letters was written from Pimlico, 13th April, 1796.

The next name mentioned in connection with the new Bishopric was that of the Rev. Philip Toosey, of Quebec, the Ecclesiastical Commissary of the Eastern District of Canada. He was strongly recommended for the position by Lord Dorchester, Governor-in-Chief, and his nomination was warmly urged by the Bishop of Nova Scotia. Thinking his success would be more certain were he in England, where his official position as Commissary would enable him to represent more fully the necessity for the establishment of the See, his friends advised him to proceed to London without delay.

So well did Mr. Toosey acquit himself in his mission, that when the matter was brought up for discussion, he not only numbered among his supporters many influential men, but even such renowned ecclesiastics as the Lord Bishop of Lincoln and His Grace the Archbishop of Canterbury.

The letters preserved among the State Papers, bearing on Mr. Toosey's visit to England, are as follows:

On the 18th of August, 1792, King wrote from Whitehall to Lieut. Governor Clarke, urgently requesting Mr. Toosey's leave of absence.*

King was informed in return that Mr. Toosey's presence might be dispensed with for the winter, but that he must be in Canada as early as possible in the spring.†

On the 13th of March, 1793, we encounter the " Memorial of Revd. Philip Toosey, Rector of Quebec,"‡ This document states that Mr. Toosey has held the office of Bishop's Commissary since 1789, without salary. He has, the paper says, an intimate knowledge of both Upper and Lower Canada, but that he has neither the power nor ability to supply the clerical needs of the different Townships applying to him. He has come to England, on the suggestion of the Bishop of Nova Scotia, in the hope that a salary and certain powers might be attached to his office, or that he might be appointed Bishop of one of the Provinces of Upper or Lower Canada, where he could organize Church establishments in the new Townships.

---

* Can. Arch., Series Q, Vol. 59-1, p. 598.
† Do., Vol. 61-1, p, 203.
‡ Do., Vol. 66, p. 273.

The Archbishop of Canterbury has promised to state the claims and wishes of the memorialist, who refers to Lord Dorchester, Governor of Canada, and General Clarke, Lieutenant Governor of Quebec, for his character.

Accompanying this memorial is a *Paper on the condition of the Church of England in Canada*,* furnished by Mr. Toosey to the Bishop of Lincoln.

"There are," it states, "six clergymen of the Church of England in Lower Canada, one at Quebec, but not a single church; the members of the Church of England worship in a Roman Catholic church, before or after the service; there are three dissenting ministers, and many Roman Catholic clergy with a Bishop and coadjutor. The Bishop's salary is small." "In Upper Canada there is neither church nor are there clergy."† "The population is all Protestant, and the country already well settled." Mr. Toosey does not believe churches will be built except there is a Bishop in the country, but the people would contribute towards the support of the church were there a Bishop on the spot to recommend it with authority.

On the 20th of April, dated at London, the Bishop of Lincoln signed a strong recommendation of Mr. Toosey for the proposed Bishopric of Quebec.‡ In this paper the statement is repeated that Mr. Toosey had served for four years as Ecclesiastical Commissary of the Bishop of Nova Scotia, without salary.

The result of these efforts on behalf of the two candidates might easily be conjectured. When governors of Provinces recommend for a vacant office each his own choice, it is unlikely that either will be appointed. A compromise seems inevitable. The conclusion speedily arrived at by the home government was that the See of Quebec was offered to Dr. Jacob Mountain, chaplain of the Bishop of Lincoln, and, after due deliberation, accepted by him.

This appointment recalls the old story, repeated in a dozen different forms, but which the writer of this sketch first saw in *Punch in the Pulpit.* The King and his chaplain, the Bishop of Lincoln, were discussing the vexed subject of the Quebec Bishopric —"Had your Majesty faith as a grain of mustard seed," said the

---

* Canadian Archives, Series Q, Vol. 66, p. 273.
† This statement is inexplicable.
‡ Canadian Archives, Series Q, Vol. 66, page 279.

Bishop, "you would say to yon Mountain (Dr. Jacob Mountain the Bishop's chaplain, visible in the distance), 'Be thou removed and cast into the See, and it should be done.'" Sixteen years ago, the Rev. Dr. Jacob J. S. Mountain pointed out in a letter to the *Montreal Gazette* that this story, based on a still older one, was without foundation. The old story was that the See of York falling vacant in the reign of George II, his Majesty consulted Dr. Mountain, Bishop of Durham, who wittily replied: " Hadst thou faith, thou wouldest say to this Mountain (at the same time laying his hand on his breast), be removed and cast into the sea (see)." His Majesty laughed heartily and complied with the hint. The Rev. Jacob J. S. Mountain pointed out that the Archbishop of York of his name had been first consecrated in the reign of James I, and his progenitors had left France more than a hundred years before those of the Bishop of Quebec, and that he was made Archbishop of York in the year 1628.

The account of the family of the first Bishop of Quebec is thus briefly related by the late Rev. Armine Mountain in his *Memoir of G. J. Mountain, third Bishop of Quebec:* " The family of Mountain is of French extraction, having emigrated to England on the revocation of the Edict of Nantes, and settled in Norfolk, where they became proprietors of a small landed estate called Thwaite Hall. It remained in their hands till about the middle of the last century. The last occupant, dying young, left two sons, the younger of whom afterwards became the first Bishop of Quebec."[*] Having graduated at Caius College, Cambridge, where he became acquainted with Pitt, whose tutor and private secretary was Dr. Tomline, afterwards Bishop of Lincoln, Jacob Mountain, in 1781, married Elizabeth Mildred Wale Kentish, of Little Bardfield Hall, Essex, soon after which he was preferred to the living of St. Andrew's, Norwich. Subsequently he was chosen by Bishop Tomline to be his examining chaplain, and presented by him to the living of Buckden in Huntingdonshire.

In 1793, when the Government decided to erect the See of Quebec, his Lordship recommended his chaplain for the appointment, which was willingly adopted. " Neither of the persons more directly concerned in this measure appears to have had reason to regret it," writes Mr. Mountain, " for we find it mentioned in Tomline's Life

---
[*] Page 9.

of Pitt, as a testimony to the wisdom of that statesman's measures, that the first Bishop of Quebec had presided over the Canadian Church ' with great honour to himself, and advantage to the concerns of his extensive Diocese'; while Dr. Tomline's own biographer, in his turn, brings forward this appointment as a proof of the Bishop's good judgment, displayed in his recommendation of Dr. Mountain."*

The Right Reverend Jacob Mountain was consecrated on the 7th of July, 1793, as the first Bishop of Quebec,† and on the 13th of August,‡ accompanied by his family, the two sisters of his wife, and the family of his brother, the new prelate embarked, and as the biographer quaintly observes, "after a voyage of thirteen weeks, the thirteen Mountains arrived at Quebec on All Saints day."§ A somewhat quaint ceremony awaited the arrival of the Bishop. We are not told that he landed under a salute of eleven guns, like the Bishop of Nova Scotia, but it is recorded that the Gallican Bishop of Quebec greeted the arrival of his Anglican brother with a well-bestowed kiss on either cheek, declaring it was high time he should come to keep his people in order."||

---

* Memoir of G. J. Mountain, p. 10.
† Do.
‡ Canadian Archives, Series Q, Vol. 66, p. 321.
§ Memoir of G. J. Mountain, p. 10.
|| Do., p 208.

CHAPTER XII.

CONCLUSION.

It is not the writer's intention to continue this sketch beyond the year 1793. It seems, however, for the sake of completeness, that some account should be given of the later doings of those whose labours have been brought prominently before us.

After the appointment of Mr. Tunstall as Assistant Minister at Montreal, Mr. Delisle, it is said, continued occasionally to preach sermons in French. He certainly was in charge of the Parish during the remaining years of his life. His death occurred at Montreal on the 30th of June, 1794.*

I regret that I have not succeeded in tracing any descendants of Mr. Delisle. There is no doubt that many exist who can give an account of his life and labours, which all readers of the early days of English Church History in Canada would find very interesting.

Mr. DeMontmollin of Quebec appears to have had three sons who survived him, Samuel, John and Yodo. His three children born at Quebec, Frances, Jane and Lewes, died in their infancy. The descendants of John, his son, are now in the Southern States. A grand-daughter of Mr. De Montmollin married Mr. Samuel Marler, whose descendants are well known in Canada. Mrs. DeMontmollin died at Nicolet, the beginning of the century, at the age of ninety years, and Mr. DeMontmollin at a still later day. He is supposed to have died at Quebec, although his burial is not recorded in the Parish Register. His last signature in the Register is as a witness to a marriage on the 9th of July, 1803.

As already related, Mrs. Veyssière died at Three Rivers on the 21st of July, 1789, at the age of fifty-six years. The descendants of her daughter, Mrs. George Dame, are still found in Canada, but Mrs. Waldro Kelly accompanied her husband and family to Ireland after the declaration of peace in 1783.

In the year 1791 we first see the name of Christiana Godson, Mr. Veyssière's second wife. It is a remarkable coincidence that he should have been the third husband of each of his wives. Christiana Godson's first husband, — Craig, has several descendants. Her

---

* Canadian Archives, Series Q, Vol. 63, p. 154.

second husband was Colonel John Morris, of the *Jersey Blues.* After his last entry in his Parish Register, at Three Rivers, Mr. Veyssière wrote in a bold hand the words frequently found at the end of incompleted works, *Finis coronat opus.* Dr. Jehoshaphat Mountain was appointed as his assistant in the year 1794, and he appears to have taken the entire duty from his first arrival, as Mr. Veyssière's name does not occur in the Register after his appointment. He died on the 26th of May, 1800, and his widow on the 6th of July, 1806. He left no children. Dr. Mountain succeeded him. There is a portrait of Mr. Veyssière, painted in England in 1767, hanging in the vestry of St. James' Church, Three Rivers.

During the summer of 1793, Mr. Doty again visited New York. Whilst there he received an invitation to become Rector of St. Anne's Church, Brooklyn, N.Y. He is supposed to have accepted this charge, as the S.P.G. Annual Report for 1797 contains this item :

" It is with concern that the Society has received information that they are deprived of the useful service of this worthy missionary, Mr. John Doty, by his removal to his native country to take charge of St. Anne's Church at Brooklyn in Long Island, in the Province of New York."

However, Mr. Doty returned in September to Sorel, and was again appointed chaplain of the 60th Regiment, which was then stationed at that post. The same year H.R.H. Prince Edward visited Sorel, and Mr. Doty had the honour of preaching before him,[*] and afterwards dined with him.[†] The *Quebec Gazette* of the 4th of July, 1793, contains this account of a Masonic celebration at Sorel at which Mr. Doty was present :

" William Henry,[‡] June 25.— Yesterday being the Anniversary of St. John the Baptist, it was celebrated by Richelieu Lodge, No. 6 A.Y.M. of the Province of Lower Canada. The Body, consisting of 22 members, went in procession to Christ Church, where a sermon was preached on the occasion by the Revd. Mr. John Doty. After dinner the King and Craft, H.R.H. Prince Edward, Grand Master of Lower Canada, the Duke of Athol, Grand Master of England, Major General Clarke, and a number of Masonic toasts were drank ; and the evening concluded with great order and harmony."[§]

---
[*] Canon Anderson's Centennial Sermon, page 8.
[†] John Doty's Diary.
[‡] The name of Sorel was changed to William Henry in 1737, in honour of the visit of H. R. H. Prince William Henry, Duke of Clarence, afterwards William IV.
[§] See the account of a similar service in 1799, in Graham's *Freemasonry in Quebec*, p. 111. It is here stated that " the Rev. Bro. Doty was a gentleman of very considerable note outside the bounds of his parish."

Conclusion.

One of Mr. Doty's sisters, Jane, married Augustus Bostwick in the year 1766 at New York, and settled eventually in Canada. His mother, accompanied by his nephew, Samuel Doty, arrived at Montreal in 1784,* to reside with him. An entry in his diary, Oct., 1795, states that his mother, eighty years of age, was at that time living at Albany. His nephew Samuel, educated by him, served during the war of 1812 as Surgeon of the 3rd Battalion M. E. He died in the West Indies in the year 1820.

Mr. Doty resigned the parish of Sorel in the year 1803, relinquished his stipend from the Society, and repaired to Three Rivers, where he resided the remainder of his life. Family afflictions and various troubles are assigned as the causes of his retirement. At Three Rivers, on the 28th of July, 1819, he married his second wife, Rachel Jeffrey, who survived him. Mr. Doty died at Three Rivers, the 23rd of November, 1841, leaving no descendants. A simple stone in the old cemetery marks the place of his burial. Mrs. Doty died at Montreal, March 1, 1860. Mr. and Mrs. Doty are still remembered by old residents of Three Rivers, who speak of them as devout and honourable gentle-folk, always bearing the dignified manners and the courtly grace of a bygone age.

It is recorded that peace and harmony were the characteristics of Mr. Stuart's extensive parish. No party spirit or faction against the Church was ever known to exist, in its whole extent from Cornwall on the East to the Mohawk settlement on the Grand River on the West. " He is described by one who knew him well as a very fine, elderly man of lofty stature and powerful frame, and of somewhat stately bearing, as conceiving himself the lineal descendant of the legitimate monarch... He was subject to occasional attacks of gout, and when the attacks came on, he walked into the lake and stood there some time to soak his shoes and stockings, and then walked at a swinging pace until they became quite dry. This he found an immediate, safe, and complete cure."†

Canniff, in his history, says : — " Stuart was about six feet four inches in height, quiet and conciliating in manner, and of a kind and benevolent character."‡ One instance of his beneficent character may here be given. Chief Justice Sir John Beverley Robinson writes of him : " He had been an intimate friend of my

* Canadian Archives, Haldimand Collection, Series B, Vol. 162, page 365.
† Eastern Canada and New Foundland, page 231.
‡ Canadian Missionary Magazine, July, 1891, page 156.

father's during the five or six years that our family lived in Kingston. My father became indebted to him in the course of some transactions about land, and had given him a bond for the amount. I well remember his coming to our house near York, a short time after my father's early and sudden death, and destroying in my mother's presence the obligations of my father, declaring that he would never consent to receive any part of the amount. Then, as he was returning, he strongly urged my mother to allow him to take me with him, that I might attend Mr. Strachan's school just opened at Kingston. I went, and spent three years in his family, treated as tenderly and kindly as if I had been his own son."*

Dr. Stuart died at Kingston, on the 15th of April, 1811. His son, Rev. George O'Kill, was the well-known Archdeacon of Toronto, and another son, the Hon. Sir James, was Chief Justice of Lower Canada.

The epitaph on Dr. Stuart's monument in St. George's Cathedral, Kingston, is as follows :—

" Sacred to the memory of the Reverend John Stuart, D.D., Missionary to the Mohawk Nation, Minister at Cataraqui (now the city of Kingston), and first Rector of St. George's Church. Born in 1740 at Paxton (Penn., U.S.), and ordained in 1770 by Dr. Terrick, Bishop of London, to the Mission of the Mohawks. Among these wild children of the forest he laboured eleven years with judgment and mildness, bringing over many to Christ; and with the aid of Joseph Brant, the celebrated Indian Chief, he translated the Gospel of St. Mark and the Book of Common Prayer. From this calm and sanctified life he was awakened by the American Revolution, but faithful to his King and country, he retired to Canada, after much suffering and loss of his worldly goods. On his arrival in Montreal he was presented with the chaplaincy of Sir John Johnson's Royal Regiment of New York. His influence with the soldiers, as with the Indians, soon manifested itself in greater order, sobriety and reverence for religion. His connection with the army was exchanged in 1785 for the pastoral charge of a congregation at Cataraqui; but he still watched over one tribe of his beloved Mohawks, settled in the Bay of Quinté. In 1789, Dr. Inglis, first Colonial Bishop of Nova Scotia, appointed him Ecclesiastical Commissary of Upper Canada, and his college of Philadelphia made him

---

* Eastern Canada and New Foundland, page 231. See this information and fuller details in Canniff's *Early Settlement of Upper Canada*, and Hawkins' *Annals of the Church in Upper Canada*.

D.D. in 1790. The last 26 years of his life were devoted to his clerical duties. In winning souls to Christ, he seldom clothed religion in her terrors, but in her character of mercy and tenderness, striving to warm the bosoms of the cold and reckless with the convictions of his heart. Nothing morose or gloomy in his views and temper impaired the moral persuasion and engaging pleasantness of his social intercourse. In the relations of life he was a shining light, a tender husband, an affectionate father, and a faithful friend. His congregation looked up to him with confidence and veneration, his brethren with reverence as their father, and the father of the Church in Upper Canada. Universally beloved, this intrepid herald of the Gospel gently fell asleep the 15th of August, 1811."

There are only a few references to Mr. Toosey, after the Establishment of the See of Quebec. On the 30th of April, 1793, there is a memorial signed by him to the effect that as the Bishopric in Canada had been given to another, it is only just that his own past services should be rewarded.* On the 25th of July, King announced to him Dr. Mountain's intention of appointing him as his Commissary, and Dundas' consent to fixing his salary at £150, this sum to be considered as doing away with all retrospective claims.† This offer was accepted by Mr. Toosey.‡ Again, on the 26th of August, he wrote to King from Bury, stating that as the frigate in which he was to take passage with the Bishop of Quebec had already sailed, he desires leave of absence to prepare for the settlement of his colony of agriculturists on his lands near Quebec.§ It was not until September, 1794, that Mr. Toosey arrived at Quebec.||

Mr. Toosey died on the 14th of September, 1797. Prescott's letter of the 4th of October, announcing the event to the Duke of Portland.¶ The only subsequent references I have seen concerning him or his affairs in Canada are the following from the *Quebec Gazette*:

From the issue of the 21st of Feb., 1799:

"On Friday, the 1st March, at the subscriber's Auction Room, will be sold such articles of Mr. Toosey's as are in Town, amongst

---

* Canadian Archives, Series O, Vol. 66, pp. 280-1.
† Do., p. 304.
‡ Do., p. 305.
§ Do., p. 306.
|| Do., Vol. 69-2, p. 485.
¶ Do., Vol. 70-2, p. 343. The entry is in the Quebec Register. His last Action the Register is a baptism on the 9th of July, 1806.

which are a handsome coach, phaeton, curricle, an English mare, some wearing apparel, and a number of valuable books, catalogues of which will be distributed previous to the sale, which will commence at one o'clock."

And from the issue of the 4th December, 1833:

"STONEHAM. This is probably the first Township in Lower Canada in which attempts were made at settlement. It is situated above fifteen miles north of Quebec, and there was an open communication by a cart-road to the old Canadian settlement at Lake St. Charles, and from thence by water nearly to the township line. The surface is mountainous and rocky, but well-timbered and watered, with some good land in the valleys. The first settlement was made by the Reverend Mr. Toosey, the Church-of-England Minister at Quebec, about forty years ago. He cleared a large extent of land at a very great cost, and built a handsome and commodious house and outhouses, in the English style, with pleasure grounds and gardens, &c., on an elevation near the River Huron, which falls into the Upper Lake St. Charles, and got a number of settlers from the North of England, who generally went away after looking at the lands. Mr. Toosey probably laid out three or four thousand pounds at this place before he returned to England a few years after the first settlement.........The house and outhouses soon fell to decay, and little trace of them now remains."

In the year 1790 Mr. Tunstall married Sarah Christie, second daughter of General Gabriel Christie, Commander of the Forces in Lower Canada. He was then Assistant-Minister of the Parish of Montreal. Mr. Delisle died on the 30th of June, 1794, and the appointment of Mr. Tunstall to the vacancy was at once proceeded with.* He remained in charge of the parish until 1801, when he resigned it, and was succeeded by Dr. Jehoshaphat Mountain. The letter of the Bishop of Nova Scotia, preserved among the records of Christ Church Cathedral, relates that Mr. Tunstall " was a modest, sensible, young man, of good learning, of unblemished character, whose voice is harmonious and strong enough when he exerts it." This letter was printed on a former page.

The Rev. James M. Tunstall died at Montreal, the 25th of December, 1840, and is buried in Mount Royal Cemetery. I am

---

* Canadian Archives, Series Q, Vol. 68, p. 154 ; Vol. 69-2, p. 385 ; Vol. 71, p. 52.

indebted to Edgar E. Roe, Esqre., of Montreal, a grandson of the Rev. Mr. Tunstall, for much of the information contained in this brief sketch.

Mr. Langhorne continued to make his headquarters at Ernestown. Of the inhabitants of the Bay of Quinté, "four-fifths," he says, "were dissenters of nine or ten different denominations." His people were scattered over a country that was more than forty miles square. He had no less than ten congregations whom he visited regularly on foot. He never kept a horse. It was his custom to sling his surplice and necessary outfit in a knapsack on his back, and to set out on his grand rounds to visit his scattered flocks. He always called upon every new family that came into the district, thus winning back many who had become estranged from the Church. Many instances are recorded of the contempt with which he regarded the comforts of life when they opposed his necessary labours. On one occasion, he failed to reach a house where he was accustomed to put up for the night, until the family had retired to their beds. Rather than disturb them he shook down some straw into a farm waggon, and made a bed for himself, where the good people found him sound asleep the next morning.

He had a practice of catechising children at every service, and teaching them their prayers in the presence of the whole congregation. He was always bold in rebuking vice, and he strictly enforced the discipline of the Church in excluding evil-livers from the Communion. Whenever he entered the house of one of his parishioners, he solemnly pronounced the old-time Benediction : *Peace be to this house and to all that dwell in it.*

As he loved the Church dearly, it may readily be understood that he mistrusted and stood aloof from all who dissented from her ways. He would not eat with their ministers, nor would he walk on the same side of the road with them. It is said that an old Presbyterian minister once offered him his horse when he was greatly fatigued, and to his astonishment received the rejoinder : " Sir, you are a promoter of schism in the flock of Christ. I cannot therefore have any intercourse with you, much less accept any favour from you." Having borne with what they long considered as evidences of a very narrow spirit in Mr. Langhorne, the dissenting teachers at last took advantage of his rough exterior and want of fluency of speech to attack him on some controverted passage henever an opportunity was presented. At first he was annoyed at this movement, but being a man of resources, he soon found a plan of meeting them. Whenever any preacher attempted to entrap him into a controversy, he would hand him a pocket edition of the Greek Testament, and ask him to read the passage in the original, and when he could not comply, Mr. Langhorne would say, "You see, my good friends, the folly of listening to a teacher who cannot read the language in which the New Testament was written." This method he found very satisfactory.

The Bishop of Nova Scotia's estimate of Mr. Langhorne was that he was "uncouth and little acquainted with the world, but a conscientious and honest man." That rugged nature which made him bathe every morning in Lake Ontario, even when the ice was two feet thick in the coldest winter days, could scarcely be expected to pass muster in the soft manners and habits of an ease-loving generation; but notwithstanding all that may be said against his want of polish, in some instances amounting almost to positive rudeness, it is said there is abundant testimony that all who ever came into actual contact with him, admitted that he was a zealous, hard-working and humble-minded follower of Christ, one who has left his mark for good in many a heart and home. Mr. Langhorne continued to serve his extensive mission until the year 1813, when he was forced to resign through ill health,[*] purposing to return to England.[†] Local tradition says he was lost at sea on the home voyage.[‡]

Dr. Samuel Peters returned to America in 1805. Sabine says he was elected first Bishop of Vermont, but declined the appointment.[§] This writer gives a very full account of Dr. Peters' life and doings, making many quotations from his letters, taken from the pages of an unsympathetic biographer. We read, " He was fully six feet high, remarkably erect, and of a large and muscular body, but not fat: his eyes were blue, and his face strongly marked by the small-pox......In his domestic and private relations, he was everything that could be desired. He loved kings, admired the British government, and revered the hierarchy. He aped the style of an English

---

[*] S. P. G. Records, p. 875.
[†] Kingston *Gazette*, March 12, 1813.
[‡] The Rev. E. H. M. Baker, Rector of Bath (Ernestown), kindly provided me with the last two references. For fuller details of Mr. Langhorne's labours, see the pages of Canniff and Hawkins.
[§] Sketches of Loyalists, p. 181.

Conclusion.

nobleman : built his house in a forest, kept a coach, and looked with some degree of scorn upon Republicans."*

He died at New York, April 19, 1826, survived by one son, who died a few years later at New Orleans, and one daughter, Hannah, who married William Jarvis, Secretary of Upper Canada.†

Reference has already been made to the Bishop of Quebec's first account to the Colonial Office of the visitation of his extensive Diocese. He found the Church, he says, in a deplorable condition. There was not one Anglican church between Montreal and Kingston, nor any place of worship, except one Lutheran and perhaps two Presbyterian. At Niagara he found a minister, but no church, and he recommends Mr. Addison for the same allowance as that given to the other missionaries. The date of this letter was the 15th September, 1794. Again, the Bishop wrote on the 6th of November, 1795, urging the Government to make Mr Addison an allowance of £150 per annum.‡ On the 26th of June, 1796, the Duke of Portland wrote to Governor Simcoe to the effect that the Bishop had asked for too large a grant, that £100 was amply sufficient, and he declared that the only men who should be sent over were clergymen with large independent means, who would require no grant from the Government.§ Again, on the 20th of February, 1798, Russell, then Lieutenant-Governor of Upper Canada, wrote to the Duke of Portland that the Bishop of Quebec has approved of Mr. Addison, as one of four clergymen to whom the Government has promised salaries.|| In one of his letters to the Bishop, the Duke of Portland gave as a reason for the delay in putting Mr. Addison's name on the clergy list, the fact that " Niagara was so shortly to be given up to the Americans!"¶ *Fort* Niagara was certainly transferred to the United States on the 11th of August, 1796 ;** but, unfortunately for His Grace's Geography, Niagara on the Canadian side of the river was not identical with Fort Niagara, which was on the American side. I do not know how long Mr. Addison was compelled to wait for the payment of his stipend, but there is an entry in the *Minutes of Executive Council on State Matters*, dated the

---
* Sketches of Loyalists, p. 182.   † Do.
‡ Can. Arch., Series Q., Vol. 74-2, p. 403.
§ Do., Vol. 282-1, page 157.
|| Do., Vol. 284, page 76.
¶ Do., Vol. 282-1, page 157.
** Do., Vol. 285, page 208.

28th of August, 1798, which suggests that this eminent divine had to turn his attention to some secular pursuit for a period. This paper recommends that the salt-springs should be leased to the Rev. Mr. Addison at five shillings a year, so long as he continues to officiate as a clergyman of the Church of England at Niagara.
At the Centenary of St. Mark's Church, the Venerable Archdeacon of Niagara stated that "Mr. Addison had been appointed to the parish in the month of June, 1791, and that as one of the three clergymen of the Church of England in Upper Canada he had a large tract of country assigned to him as a travelling missionary, extending from York (Toronto) in the East, to London in the West. He was appointed by Governor Simcoe chaplain of the Provincial Parliament, the first session of which was held at the town of Niagara." "I myself," to quote again from Dr. Scadding's paper, "remember Mr. Addison very well. When a boy, I have heard him repeatedly officiate in St. James' Church at York. His oval, intellectual countenance and finished style of reading made a strong impression. In addition, I particularly remember observing him as he walked arrayed in his academic gown, bands, and clerical hat, from the church after the service. . . Mr. Addison built a house for himself, styled by him 'Lake Lodge,' on some property acquired close to the town of Niagara, wherein, as might be expected from his scholarly instincts, a library soon accumulated around him, a considerable portion of which is still preserved as an heir-loom in the parsonage attached to St. Mark's Church. We have in this library a deposit of the solid Divinity common in English parsonages some sixty years since, including works by Warburton, Walter Land, Jeremy Taylor, John Jackson, Leslie, and so forth. Voluminous folio copies of Pool's *Synopsis*, Bayle's *Critical Dictionary*, and Clarendon's *History of the Great Rebellion*, all likewise seem here to be remarkably in place. There is to be noted also a black-letter quarto folio copy of the Geneva version of the Bible with the Liturgy attached of the time of Charles the First." The late Bishop Strachan, of Toronto, said of Mr. Addison, in 1840: "He was a gentleman of commanding talents and exquisite wit, whose devotedness to his sacred duties, kindliness of manners, and sweet companionship, are still sources of grateful and fond remembrance. He may justly be considered the missionary of the western part of the Province. In every township we find traces of his ministrations, and endearing recollections of his affectionate visits." Dr. Scadding

continues: "With great appropriateness, at his decease in 1829, the mortal remains of Mr. Addison were deposited under the chancel of St. Mark's Church."

Having laboured faithfully for thirty-seven years in the parish of Niagara, Mr. Addison was called to his rest on the 6th of October, 1829, at the age of seventy-five years. The tablet on the wall of St. Mark's Church bears the inscription:

"In memory of Rev. Robert Addison, first missionary of this District, of the venerable the Society for the Propagation of the Gospel in Foreign Parts. He commenced his labours in 1792, which by the blessing of Divine Providence he was enabled to continue for thirty-seven years. Besides his stated services as minister of St. Mark's in the town, he visited and officiated in different parts of this and adjoining Districts until other missionaries arrived. 'Remember them which have the rule over you.'"

THE END.

www.ingramcontent.com/pod-product-compliance
Lightning Source LLC
Chambersburg PA
CBHW022143160426
43197CB00009B/1413